Lecture Notes in Economics and Mathematical Systems 457

Springer
Berlin
Heidelberg
New York
Barcelona
Budapest
Hong Kong
London
Milan
Paris
Santa Clara
Singapore
Tokyo

Chiente Hsu

Volume and the Nonlinear Dynamics of Stock Returns

 Springer

332.6322
H87v

Author

Dr. Chiente Hsu
University of Vienna
Department of Economics
Hohenstaufengasse 9
A-1010 Vienna, Austria

Library of Congress Cataloging-in-Publication Data

Hsu, Chiente, 1964-
    Volume and the nonlinear dynamics of stock returns / Chiente Hsu.
        p.   cm. -- (Lecture notes in economics and mathematical
    systems, ISSN 0075-8442 ; 457)
        Includes bibliographical references (p.   ).
        ISBN 3-540-63672-2 (acid-free paper)
        1. Stocks--Prices--Mathematical models. 2. Return on investment.
    I. Title.   II. Series.
    HG4636.H78   1998
    332.63'222--dc21   97-35146
                                                                       CIP

ISSN 0075-8442
ISBN 3-540-63672-2 Springer-Verlag Berlin Heidelberg New York

© Springer-Verlag Berlin Heidelberg 1998
Printed in Germany

The use of general descriptive names, registered names, trademarks, etc. in this
publication does not imply, even in the absence of a specific statement, that such
names are exempt from the relevant protective laws and regulations and therefore
free for general use.

Typesetting: Camera ready by author
SPIN: 10549323   42/3142-543210 - Printed on acid-free paper
JK

Preface

This manuscript is about the joint dynamics of stock returns and trading volume. It grew out of my attempt to construct an intertemporal asset pricing model with rational agents which can explain the relation between volume, volatility and persistence of stock return documented in empirical literature. Most part of the manuscript is taken from my thesis. I wish to express my deep appreciation to Peter Kugler and Benedikt Pöetscher, my advisors of the thesis, for their invaluable guidance and support. I wish to thank Gerhard Orosel and Gerhard Sorger for their encouraging and helpful discussions. Finally, my thanks go to George Tauchen who has been generous in giving me the benefit of his numerical and computational experience, in providing me with programs and in his encouragement.

Contents

1
Introduction

The central idea of efficient stock markets is that stock prices are determined by the interaction of self-interested profit maximizing rational agents. Models of competitive equilibrium imply that marginal revenue from an activity equals its marginal cost. As the cost of reproduction of publicly available information is zero, the expected returns should also amount to zero. The knowledge that a certain firm will do well in the future does not imply that its stock should be bought now, since the price of this firm's stock will be bid to the point where no extra capital gain on the stock will occur when the high earnings actually materialize. In his classic survey, Fama [22] defined an efficient stock market as one in which stock prices "fully reflect" all available information.

The efficiency of stock markets provides traders with a convenient means of hedging risks. In such a circumstance no investor or speculator can earn extraordinary profits by exploiting publicly available information. However, if stock markets are informationally efficient in that current prices incorporate all information, any pervasive activity on volume data analysis is pointless since one would not expect to observe a causal relationship

between volume and stock prices at all. The widely held belief
that price and volume data provide indicators of future price
movements therefore seems to be at odds with the hypothesis
of an efficient stock market. However, the development of the
stock market in the late 1980s has been characterized by sharp
price movements accompanied by high volume. On October 19,
1987, the S&P 500 composite index plunged 22.9 percent on
the second highest volume ever recorded. On the day after the
crash, the S&P 500 index rose by 5.2 percent with the highest
trading volume ever recorded. On October 13, 1989, the index
dropped 7 percent accompanied by a 50 percent increase in volume and followed by heavy trading two and a half times the
normal volume on the next trading day.[1]

This manuscript is about returns and volume on stock markets. We undertake a theoretical as well as an empirical investigation of the dynamic interrelationships between price and volume movements on the stock markets. There are two reasons
why the return-volume relation is important. First, it provides
insight into the structure of financial markets. Different economic models, some of which will be discussed here, predict
different return-volume relations that depend on the degree and
nature of heterogeneity among investors. For example, there is
now considerable evidence that the expected return on the aggregate stock market varies over time. Morse [57] explains this
by constructing a model in which traders have diverse information. Periods of high volume are periods when traders' information is more diverse and is in the process of converging.
During these periods learning takes place, beliefs converge and
correlations of return are induced by this convergence mechanism. Morse's model implies a positive relation between trading
volume and persistence of return.[2]

The other explanation of time-varying expected return is that
it results from the interaction between different groups of in-

---

[1] This is taken from Gallant, Rossi and Tauchen [32].

[2] In more recent work, Antoniewicz [2] documents increases in correlation on higher
trading volume for a number of individual firms which are consistent with Morse's results,
indicating more persistence when trading volume is high.

vestors. Suppose that some investors desire to sell stock for exogenous reasons (i.e. non-informational trading). Other investors are risk-averse utility maximizers; they are willing to accommodate the fluctuations in non-informational traders' demand for stock only if they are rewarded with a higher expected return. This implies that there will tend to be price increases on subsequent days. Thus the model with non-informational trade predicts the autocorrelation of returns to be smaller on high volume days. Empirical relations between returns and volume can help discriminate between different hypotheses about the different nature of heterogeneity among traders.

Second, the return-volume relation is crucial to the empirical distribution of stock returns. It is well known that high frequency financial data exhibit time-varying conditional heteroskedasticity. One property of stock market volatility relates to the persistence of shocks to the variance. It has been found by many researchers that the null hypothesis of a unit root in the conditional variance is typically not rejected.[3] The finding of a unit root seems robust to the parameterization of the ARCH model chosen. In searching for the origins of the ARCH effects, Lamoureux and Lastrapes [45] argue that the ARCH effect is a manifestation of clustering in trading volumes. By introducing the contemporaneous trading volumes into the conditional variance equation, they find that the lagged squared residuals are no longer significant.

A large amount of empirical as well as theoretical work has been done on the price-volume relationship. On the one hand, however, the previous empirical work tends to be exclusively data-based and is not guided by equilibrium models of market behavior. The models are more statistical than economic in character. On the other hand, most of existing theoretical models in which trade is generated by heterogeneous agents and incomplete markets do not confront the data in its full complexity. There seems to be no model with dynamically optimizing heterogeneous agents that can jointly account for the major styl-

---

[3]See Bollerslev, Chou and Kroner [7] for a survey.

ized facts of the return-volume relation. The major theme of this manuscript is to investigate the extent to which a simple intertemporal asset pricing model with non-informational trading can account for the observed joint dynamics of stock returns and trading volume in the stock markets.

The plan of this manuscript is as follows: Chapter 2 provides a brief review of theoretical and empirical literature dealing with stock market efficiency. Two empirical findings are often taken as evidence against the efficient market hypothesis: (i) the significant autocorrelations in stock returns and (ii) the excess volatility in stock prices. However, tests of the efficient market hypothesis are joint tests of an equilibrium model of expected returns and rational processing of available information by investors. The negative empirical results of the efficient market hypothesis also suggest that traditional models of return determination cannot successfully explain these stylized facts.

In Chapter 3, we take a critical view of the asset pricing models in which agents have rational expectations but are different with respect to information available to them. We argue that these models cannot explain the informational content of volume data. We propose an alternative model with nontradable asset. The model is a fully dynamic one in which agents have rational expectations and are heterogeneous with respect to their investment opportunity. We propose that the shocks in the economy have deterministic but time-varying volatility. We show that there is a rational expectations equilibrium in which the market clearing price is linear in the returns of the risky assets in the economy. We further show analytically that the predicted relation between the serial correlation of stock returns and volume is not monotonic: it can be positive or negative, depending on the probability structure of the shocks. This result can explain the controversial findings in empirical literature studying the relation between volume and the persistence of stock returns. The relation between volume and volatility is more complicated and cannot be derived analytically. Thus, we rely on the numerical exercises.

In Chapter 4 we present numerical evidence that this economy can mimic the stochastic volatility properties of financial returns. This suggests that the assumption of deterministic volatility might be a reasonable first approximation. In the simulations to be reported in Chapter 4, we model the deterministic volatility process by the chaotic tent map dynamics which is known to behave similar as an AR(1) process (Sakai and Tokumaru, [63]). The simulated stock return mimics the GARCH behavior quite well. Thus, modelling the volatility as an autocorrelated time-varying deterministic process can be viewed as an approximation to the ARCH or GARCH process (Engle, [18], Bollerslev, [7]) which is one of the most prominent tools for characterizing changing variance of financial time series. The ambiguous relation between the serial correlation of stock return and volume as well as the positive relation between volume and the volatility of stock return are confirmed in a series of empirical and numerical examples. Therefore, the data generated from the simple dynamic asset pricing model with a time-varying volatility can mimic the volume-persistence and volume-volatility relation revealed in the observed data well.

In Chapter 5 we undertake an empirical investigation of the joint dynamics of stock returns and volume using nonparametric methods. The empirical effort is exclusively data-based. The data used here comprises the daily Dow Jones Industrial Average and the number of shares traded daily on the New York Stock Exchange from January 1, 1952 through September 30, 1987. We first provide a brief review of empirical stylized facts about stock returns and volume. We then apply a semi nonparametric method as suggested by Gallant and Tauchen [32] to estimate the bivariate conditional density of stock return and trading volume. We also utilize a non-linear impulse response technique developed by Gallant, Rossi and Tauchen [33] to investigate the joint dynamics of the two series.

In Chapter 6 the asset pricing model with nontradable asset proposed in Chapter 3 is estimated and tested by applying the Efficient Method of Moments (EMM) estimator by Gallant and Tauchen [34]. The same data set as in Chapter 5 is used to investigate the implications of the structural model. We examine which of the characteristics seen in the data can be described by this simple asset pricing model and which cannot. Conclusions and a short discussion of as yet unresolved issues are presented in Chapter 7.

2
Efficient Stock Markets

This chapter is a review of the theoretical and empirical literature that studies stock market efficiency. At the outset it is important to note that any test of market efficiency is in fact a joint test of several hypotheses, i.e., tests of the efficient market hypothesis in the stock market are necessarily joint tests of an equilibrium model of expected returns and of rational processing of available information by investors. One specifies a model of equilibrium expected returns and an information set for the investors, and one postulates that economic agents set asset prices to make expected returns on assets conform to the expected values predicted by the model.[1] If the hypothesis of efficiency is rejected, it could be because the market is inefficient or because an incorrect equilibrium model has been assumed.

This chapter begins by looking at two theoretical models of determination of stock prices: the martingale model by Samuelson [64] and the consumption-based asset pricing model by Lucas [52]. Both models provide analytical frameworks to test the efficient market hypothesis. Section 2 discusses various empiri-

---

[1] Fama writes ([23], p. 168), "Formal tests require formal models, with their more or less unrealistic structuring of the world."

cal tests that seek to assess the efficiency of stock markets. The empirical work is divided into three categories: (1) autocorrelation based tests, (2) volatility tests and (3) tests based on time-varying expected returns. The literature on volatility tests is surveyed in greater detail, since these tests are among the first anomalies which are widely accepted as evidence against the efficient market hypothesis and powerful examples of the importance of stationarity assumptions. Furthermore, they are also the first widely used rational expectations tests that take into account unobserved investor information.

2.1   Equilibrium Models of Asset Pricing

2.1.1   The Martingale Model of Stock Prices

In his 1965 work, Paul Samuelson [64] develops the link between market efficiency and martingales. A stochastic process y_t is a martingale with respect to a sequence of σ-fields I_t if y_t is I_t-measurable and if it has the property

$$E(y_{t+1}|I_t) = y_t. \tag{2.1}$$

If y_t is a martingale, its first difference $x_t \equiv y_t - y_{t-1}$ can be viewed as the payoff from a fair game in the sense that

$$E(x_{t+1}|I_t) = 0. \tag{2.2}$$

Denote the return on a stock as

$$r_{t+1} \equiv \frac{p_{t+1} + d_{t+1}}{p_t} - 1$$

where p_t is the stock price and d_t the dividends on the stock. In the context of the stock market, the unpredictability of stock returns is equivalent to the rate of return r_t less a constant γ being a fair game, i.e.,

$$E(r_{t+1} - \gamma|I_t) = E(\frac{p_{t+1} + d_{t+1} - p_t}{p_t} - \gamma|I_t) = 0, \tag{2.3}$$

where I_t is assumed to comprise at least historical prices and dividends. If returns on a stock are a fair game, the stock price p_t is given by

$$p_t = \beta E(p_{t+1} + d_{t+1}|I_t), \qquad (2.4)$$

with $\beta = 1/(1+\gamma)$.

Equation (2.4) says that the stock price today equals the sum of the expected future price and dividends, discounted back to the present at a rate β. Substituting recursively for p_{t+1}, p_{t+2}, etc. into (2.4) and applying the law of iterated expectations results in

$$p_t = E(\sum_{i=1}^{n} \beta^i d_{t+i} + \beta^n p_{t+n}|I_t). \qquad (2.5)$$

Suppose the transversality condition

$$\lim_{n \to \infty} \beta^n E(p_{t+n}|I_t) = 0 \qquad (2.6)$$

holds, then

$$p_t = E(\sum_{i=1}^{\infty} \beta^i d_{t+i}|I_t). \qquad (2.7)$$

Therefore, Samuelson's result shows that the fair game model (2.3) plus rational expectations imply that stock prices equal the sum of the expected present value of future dividends. The present value model (2.7) forms the testable efficient market hypothesis which most of the volatility tests, surveyed in section 2.2, rely on.

2.1.2 Lucas' Consumption Based Asset Pricing Model

The martingale model described above does not spell out complete general equilibrium setups: Neither the optimization problem agents face nor the information structure is specified. It leaves open the exact way in which the economy is imagined to fit together, say, to yield the constant rate of return as assumed in the martingale model. Lucas' consumption-based asset-pricing model (Lucas [52]) was one of the first models developed from the maximizing behavior of a representative agent in an infinite horizon environment which allows for risk aversion as well as risk neutrality. It is a complete, dynamic, general equilibrium model that provides useful insights into the nature of risk premium in asset markets.

Lucas imagines an economy consisting of a large number of agents that are identical with respect to their preferences and endowments. The representative consumer maximizes the expectation of a time-separable life time utility

$$\max_{c} E\left[\sum_{t=0}^{\infty} \beta^t u(c_t) \mid I_0\right], \qquad 0 < \beta < 1, \qquad (2.8)$$

$$\text{subject to } A_{t+1} = R_t(A_t + y_t - c_t)$$

with A_0 given. Here I_0 denotes the information set agents have at the beginning of time 0^2, $u(c_t)$ is the agent's instantaneous utility function depending on the consumption at time t, β is the discount factor, y_t is the agent's labor income, A_t is the amount of the asset valued in units of the consumption good, held at the beginning of period t and R_t is the real gross rate of return on the asset between dates t and $t+1$, measured in units of $t+1$ consumption good per time t consumption good. In general, $\{R_t\}$ is a random process and R_t becomes known to the agent only at the beginning of period $t+1$. The Euler equation for this maximization problem then is

$$u'(c_t) = E\left[\beta R_t u'(c_{t+1}) \mid I_t\right], \qquad t = 0, 1, \dots \qquad (2.9)$$

where I_t denotes the information set agents have at the beginning of time t, $u'(c_t)$ and $u'(c_{t+1})$ are the marginal utilities.[3]

---

[2] So, I_0 contains A_0 and y_0.

[3] Special cases of the Euler equation (2.9) provide the basis for several theories, for example Hall's (1978) random walk theory of consumption in which R_t is assumed to be constant and is a risk-free rate of return, so that $R_t = R$ for all t. Then (2.9) implies that $E_t u'(c_{t+1}) = (\beta R)^{-1} u'(c_t)$ which is Hall's result that the marginal utility of consumption follows a univariate first-order Markov process and that no other variables

Suppose $y_t = 0$ for all t, and the only durable good in the economy is a set of "trees" (stocks), which are equal in number to the agents in the economy. Each period, each tree yields fruit or dividends to the amount of d_t to its owner at the beginning of period t. We assume that d_t is governed by a Markov process, with time-invariant transition density $f(x', x)$ where $prob\{d_{t+1} \leq x' \mid d_t = x\} = \int_0^{x'} f(s, x)\,ds$. Thus the conditional expectations in (2.9) will eventually be defined with respect to this transition probability. Each agent is endowed with one tree and its initial dividend at time zero. Let p_t be the price of a tree in period t, measured in units of consumption goods per tree. With $R_t = (p_{t+1} + d_{t+1})/p_t$ in (2.9), the equilibrium prices satisfy

$$u'(c_t)p_t = E\left[\beta u'(c_{t+1})(p_{t+1} + d_{t+1}) \mid I_t\right]. \qquad (2.10)$$

The interpretation of equation (2.10) is the following: suppose an investor is considering selling one share of her stock and consuming the proceeds. The utility gain is $u'(c_t)p_t$. The budget constraint implies a drop in consumption at $t+1$ of $p_{t+1} + d_{t+1}$. The RHS of equation (2.10) yields the expected utility cost of the decline in consumption, discounted back to t. At his optimum, the agent's utility gain at t must equal the expected utility loss at $t+1$.

In this economy, however, we must, in equilibrium, have $c_t = d_t$, because all consumers are identical and $u(.)$ is strictly increasing, and there is only one source of goods, this period's dividends. Substituting $c_t = d_t$ in (2.10) and rearranging the equation, we have

$$p_t = E\left[\beta \frac{u'(d_{t+1})}{u'(d_t)}(p_{t+1} + d_{t+1}) \mid I_t\right]. \qquad (2.11)$$

---

in the information set help to predict (Granger cause) $u'(c_{t+1})$, once lagged $u'(c_t)$ has been included.

Using recursions on (2.11) and the law of iterated expectations, we find that one solution of (2.11) is

$$p_t = E\left[\sum_{i=0}^{\infty} \beta^i \frac{u'(d_{t+i})}{u'(d_t)} d_{t+i} \mid I_t\right], \qquad (2.12)$$

which is a generalization of (2.7) in which the share price is an expected discounted stream of dividends but with time-varying and stochastic discount rates.[4] Since for any two random variables x, y, it is always true that

$$E(xy \mid I_t) = E(x \mid I_t) E(y \mid I_t) + \text{cov}(x, y \mid I_t),$$

where

$$\text{cov}(x, y \mid I_t) \equiv E\left\{[x - E(x \mid I_t)][y - E(y \mid I_t)] \mid I_t\right\},$$

equation (2.11) can be rewritten as

$$
\begin{aligned}
1 &= E\left[\beta \frac{u'(d_{t+1})}{u'(d_t)} \frac{p_{t+1} + d_{t+1}}{p_t} \mid I_t\right] \qquad (2.13) \\
&= \beta E\left[\frac{u'(d_{t+1})}{u'(d_t)} \mid I_t\right] E\left(\frac{p_{t+1} + d_{t+1}}{p_t} \mid I_t\right) + \\
&\quad \beta \text{cov}\left[\frac{u'(d_{t+1})}{u'(d_t)} \frac{p_{t+1} + d_{t+1}}{p_t} \mid I_t\right].
\end{aligned}
$$

If $E[u'(c_{t+1})/u'(c_t) \mid I_t]$ evaluated at $c_t = d_t$ is a constant and

$$\text{cov}\left[\frac{u'(c_{t+1})}{u'(c_t)}, \frac{p_{t+1} + d_{t+1}}{p_t} \mid I_t\right] = 0,$$

---

[4]The general solution of (2.11) is

$$p_t = E\left[\sum_{i=0}^{\infty} \beta^i \frac{u'(d_{t+i})}{u'(d_t)} d_{t+i} \mid I_t\right] + g_t \beta^{-t}.$$

for any random process g_t that obays $g_t = \beta E\left[\frac{u'(d_{t+1})}{u'(d_t)} g_{t+1} \mid I_t\right]$. However, equation (2.12) is the only solution which satisfies the transversality condition

$$\lim_{n \to \infty} \beta^n E(p_{t+n} \mid I_t) = 0.$$

If $g_t \neq 0$, $g_t \beta^{-t}$ fails to converge as $t \to \infty$ because $0 < \beta < 1$. The proof is given in, for example, Sargent [65], Appendix pp. 345-347.

equation (2.13) implies that

$$p_t = \beta\gamma E(p_{t+1} + d_{t+1}|I_t)$$

with $\gamma \equiv E\left[u'(c_{t+1})/u'(c_t) \mid I_t\right]$. Therefore, p_t is a martingale. This is true if $u(c_t)$ is linear in c_t, so that agents are risk neutral. In this case, equation (2.12) reduces to the constant-return present-value model (2.7). Therefore, the martingale property holds for p_t if agents are risk neutral.

2.2   Econometric Tests of the Efficient Markets Hypothesis

This section discusses various empirical tests that seek to assess the efficiency of stock markets. As mentioned above, it is important to keep in mind that any test of market efficiency is a joint test of several hypotheses. It is insoluble to date to develop a direct test of the hypothesis that the stock market is efficient. All that can be done is to present various equilibrium models of expected returns regarding what one means by market efficiency and test these specifications by placing additional assumptions on the statistical properties of the data. Hence, "*market efficiency per se is not testable. It must be tested jointly with some model of equilibrium, an asset-pricing model.*" (Fama, [24]). For example, Fama [22] argues that an efficient market is a market where prices "fully reflect" all available information. In such a circumstance no investor can earn extraordinary profits by exploiting publicly available information. This does not imply that, in equilibrium, expected return on an stock is constant through time. Tests of market efficiency are necessarily joint tests of an equilibrium model of expected returns and rational processing of available information by investors. Rejection of the null hypothesis is consequently not necessarily to be identified with market inefficiency. Since it is possible that an incorrect equilibrium model has been assumed.

The statistical problem that plagues studies of the efficient market is that certain statistical properties must be assumed for the time series used in the analysis. A misspecified statistical model renders the results of the tests on the efficient market hypothesis inappropriate. The development of literature on volatility tests is one of the best example of this problem and is illustrated below.

2.2.1 Autocorrelation Based Tests

The early (pre-1970) empirical literature on testing of stock market efficiency concentrates on the test of the hypothesis that expected returns are constant through time. Market efficiency then implies that returns are unpredictable at least from past returns, and the best forecast of a return is its sample mean. Nonzero correlations would suggest that stock markets are not informationally efficient.

The early tests often find suggestive evidence that daily, weekly and monthly returns are predictable from past returns. For example, Fama [21] finds that the first-order autocorrelations of daily returns are positive for 23 out of the 30 Dow Jones Industrials and more than 2 standard errors from 0 for 11 of the 30. Fisher [26] finds that the autocorrelations of monthly returns on diversified portfolios are positive and larger than those for individual stocks.

An example of the more recent work in estimating autocorrelation in daily and weekly returns is the paper by Lo and MacKinlay [50]. They use daily data on NYSE and AMEX stocks back to 1962 and find that weekly returns on portfolios of NYSE stocks grouped according to size (stock price times shares outstanding) have positive autocorrelation coefficients in the order of 0.3. In addition, the autocorrelation is stronger for portfolios of small stocks. French and Roll [27] also find that the first-order autocorrelation of daily returns on the individual stocks of large NYSE firms are positive. In short, with daily data back to 1962, recent research has been able to show confidently that daily and weekly returns are predictable from the past returns. The work thus rejects the market efficiency-constant expected returns model on a statistical basis.

The more striking evidence on the predictability of returns from past returns comes from long-horizon returns, in most cases multi-year returns. Fama and French [25] estimate directly the correlation between average returns over the interval from $t - T$ to t - denoted as $r_{t-T,t}$ - with $r_{t,t+T}$ for various values of T. In contrast to the positive serial correlation in daily, weekly and monthly returns documented in previous studies, they find a $U-$shaped pattern of autocorrelations of diversified portfolios of NYSE stocks for the 1926-1985 period: For T of one year the correlation is almost zero. For T in the order of three to five years about 35 percent of the variation in $r_{t,t+T}$ is explained by $r_{t-T,t}$. For T of ten years the correlation reverts to approximately zero. Porterba and Summers [60] find negative serial correlation for 96 month returns of the value-weighted CRSP NYSE index from 1926 to 1985. These findings lead many researchers to raise the question: What kind of model would generate the U- shaped pattern in the return autocorrelations that Fama and French reported? Shiller [69] and Summers [71] propose that instead of modeling stock price as a martingale, one should consider assuming that price comprises a random walk plus a slowly mean-reverting stationary series. This specification generates exactly the U-pattern observed in the data. An example is[5]:

$$
\begin{aligned}
\ln d_t &= \mu + \ln d_{t-1} + \epsilon_t, && (2.14) \\
\ln p_t &= \tau + \ln d_t + a_t, \\
a_t &= \phi a_{t-1} + \nu_t,
\end{aligned}
$$

where ϵ_t and ν_t are uncorrelated white noises. The mean log price-dividend ratio τ is perturbed by an AR(1) random variable a_t with $|\phi| < 1$. In the spirit of Shiller and Summer, a_t is interpreted as "fads", i.e., optimistic or pessimistic waves which influence investors expectations that drive the stock price away from the fundamental value. Most efficient-markets critics now emphasize a "fads" interpretation of the rejection of the

---

[5] West [78].

market-efficiency hypothesis. In a fad, the price deviates from
the present value of future dividends, due to noise or feedback
trading, irrational expectations, or some other inefficiency.

The evidence on the long-run predictability of return seemed
striking at first, but the results turn out to be not robust: When
Fama and French delete the 1926-1940 period from the tests,
the evidence of strong negative autocorrelations in 3- to 5-years
returns disappears. Furthermore, Kim, Nelson and Startz [43]
find evidence of mean reversion only in data sets that include
the 1930s, whereas for the post World War II period they find
no evidence of negative return autocorrelation. Moreover, the
extremely small sample size (from 1926 to 1985 there are only
12 nonoverlapping five-year returns) provides good reason to
be wary of such inferences. By properly adjusting for the small
sample sizes and for other statistical issues associated with long-
horizon returns, Richardson and Stock [62] and Richardson [61]
reverse many of the inferences of Fama and French [25] and
Porterba and Summers [60].

2.2.2   Volatility Tests

In the early 90's, it was realized that Samuelson's martingale
model, which implies that returns should be unforecastable, also
implies that stock prices should have a volatility which is low
relative to the volatility of dividends. Defining the discounted
sum of future dividends as "ex-post rational prices" of a stock
(Shiller, [68]), equation (2.7) can be written as

$$p_t = E(p_t^*|I_t), \qquad (2.15)$$

with

$$p_t^* = \sum_{i=1}^{\infty} \beta^i d_{t+i}, \qquad (2.16)$$

where I_t is the information set comprising all information available to the market at time t. Thus the stock price p_t is the
conditional expectation of its "ex-post rational prices" p_t^*. Since

the variance of the conditional expectation of a random variable is less than or equal to the variance of the random variable itself, we have

$$\frac{\text{Var}(p_t)}{\text{Var}(p_t^*)} \leq 1, \tag{2.17}$$

if the unconditional variances exist. This is the simplest form of the so-called "variance-bound" inequality. LeRoy and Porter [49] and Shiller [68] estimate (2.17) using different techniques to calculate the ratio. Both of them find stock market volatility to be far greater than could be justified by the underlying present-value model.

Econometric Flaws of the Early Volatility Tests: Unit Root Problem

Shortly after both LeRoy/Porter's and Shiller's papers were published, these variance-bounds tests were found to be subject to certain econometric problems. One of the most serious problems of the early volatility tests lies in the assumption of the stationarity of p_t and d_t. If the variables have unit roots, then the variances are functions of time. Any sample variance is not a good estimator of the corresponding population variance. Kleidon [44] runs Monte Carlo studies in which the present-value relation holds by construction and using a geometric random walk model for dividends[6]

$$ln(d_{t+1}) = ln(d_t) + \epsilon_{t+1}, \tag{2.18}$$

where ϵ_t is distributed independently as normal with mean μ and variance σ^2. It is assumed that $\mu + \sigma^2/2 = 0$ so that $E(d_{t+i}|d_t, d_{t-1,...}) = d_t$ and, hence, d_t is a martingale. Suppose agents form their expectation based on the information set containing past dividends. Prices are generated by

$$p_t = \sum_{i=1}^{\infty} \beta^i E(d_{t+i}|d_t, d_{t-1}, ...). \tag{2.19}$$

---

[6]Kleidon [44], Proposition 4, p. 964.

If dividends follow the process as in equation (2.18), the implied price is then

$$p_t = \frac{\beta}{1-\beta} d_t. \tag{2.20}$$

so that p_t is a martingale as well. Define a statistic θ with

$$\theta = \frac{\sum_{t=1}^{T}(p_t^*)^2}{T} - \frac{\sum_{t=1}^{T}p_t^2}{T}, \tag{2.21}$$

then $E(\theta) > 0$ in the model considered. However, conducted on simulated data, Kleidon finds that, following Shiller's (Shiller [68]) detrending procedure, the estimate for $E(\theta)$ violates the inequality $E(\theta) > 0$ with a frequency of approximately 90 percent. He argues that the detrending procedure Shiller, LeRoy and Porter applied to the series produces a stationary series only if the original series is trend stationary. As a consequence, a violation of a stationary assumption leads to bias against the acceptance of efficiency and the interpretation of the test results as a rejection of present-value model for stocks is not warranted. This leaves open the question of whether these econometric flaws are so large as to explain the entire excess of $\text{Var}(p_t)$ over $\text{Var}(p_t^*)$.

Marsh and Merton [54] provide an example to address the problem associated with unit root: Suppose that a firm's managers set the firm's dividend equal to a constant fraction of its stock price last period, i.e.,

$$d_{t+1} = \delta + p_t \tag{2.22}$$

where there is a unique constant δ which satisfies equation (2.15). It can be shown that both dividends and prices follow unit root processes in this example: Substitute (2.22) into (2.16) the expost rational price p_t^* can be written as

$$p_t^* = (1-\beta) \sum_{i=0}^{\infty} \beta^i p_{t+i}$$

which is a smoothed version of the actual stock price p_t, so its variance depends on the variance and autocorrelations of p_t.

Since autocorrelations can never be greater than one, p_t^* must have a lower variance than p_t. Therefore, the variance inequality (2.17) will always be violated in this example, no matter the population variances are well defined or not.

Second Round Volatility Tests

Nonstationarity does not invalidate the variance-bounds inequality. It is the assumption that these variances are constant over time - adopted in the econometric implementation of the variance bounds test - which is violated if stationarity fails. After the criticism raised by Kleidon, Marsh and Merton , there has been a large number of papers analyzing or developing volatility tests which explicitly allow for unit roots. In the following the empirical work by West [79], Mankiw, Romer and Shapiro [53] and Campbell and Shiller [13] are discussed.

West's Inequality

West [79] proposed a different approach to testing for excess volatility which is (i) valid when dividends have unit roots and (ii) does not require a proxy for p_t^*. Define

$$x_{H,t} \equiv \sum_{i=1}^{\infty} \beta^i E(d_{t+i}|H_t)$$

and

$$x_{I,t} \equiv \sum_{i=1}^{\infty} \beta^i E(d_{t+i}|I_t),$$

where H_t is the information set consisting of current and past dividends and I_t is the investors' actual information set. Assume that I_t contains H_t, the innovation variance of $x_{H,t}$ should exceed that of $x_{I,t}$

$$E\left[x_{H,t+1} - E\left(x_{H,t+1} \mid H_t\right) \mid H_t\right]^2 \qquad (2.23)$$
$$\geq \quad E\left[x_{I,t+1} - E\left(x_{I,t+1} \mid I_t\right) \mid I_t\right]^2$$

West assumes that dividends follows an autoregressive model or an integrated autoregressive model. Equation (2.23) can be applied to the data by estimating a forecasting model for dividends and computing from the model the implied $E[x_{H,t+1} - E(x_{H,t+1} \mid H_t) \mid H_t^2]$. West finds that this variance inequality is strongly violated with Standard and Poor composite stock price data using simple autoregressive models for dividends.

Mankiw, Romer and Shapiro: MRS Statistics

Mankiw, Romer and Shapiro (MRS) [53] recognize that in an efficient market the price of an asset must equal the discounted conditional expected payoff from holding the asset for k periods and reselling it:

$$p_t = E(p_t^{*k} \mid I_t), \tag{2.24}$$

with

$$p_t^{*k} = \sum_{i=1}^{k-1} \beta^i d_{t+i} + \beta^k p_{t+k}.$$

Since p_t is the optimal forecast of p_t^{*k}, this implies that $p_t^{*k} - p_t$ should be uncorrelated with any variable which is in the information set I_t. In particular, let p_t^o denote some "naive forecast" of p_t^{*k} – that is, any function of investors' information, however inaccurate as a forecast of p_t^{*k}. Since p_t^o is available at time t, it follows that

$$E\left[(p_t^{*k} - p_t)(p_t - p_t^o) \mid I_t\right] = 0 \tag{2.25}$$

if equation (2.24) holds. This in turn implies that

$$E[(p_t^{*k} - p_t^o)^2 \mid I_t] = E[(p_t^{*k} - p_t)^2 \mid I_t] + E[(p_t - p_t^o)^2 \mid I_t]. \tag{2.26}$$

The same relation holds if we normalize the data by information available at time t. Especially, divide both sides by p_t^2 in the above equation,

$$E[(\frac{p_t^{*k}}{p_t} - \frac{p_t^o}{p_t})^2 \mid I_t] = E[(\frac{p_t^{*k}}{p_t} - 1)^2 \mid I_t] + E[(1 - \frac{p_t^o}{p_t})^2 \mid I_t]. \tag{2.27}$$

Define the test statistic q_t as

$$q_t = (\frac{p_t^{*k}}{p_t} - \frac{p_t^o}{p_t})^2 - (\frac{p_t^{*k}}{p_t} - 1)^2 - (1 - \frac{p_t^o}{p_t})^2. \qquad (2.28)$$

The null hypothesis from equation (3.13) is then $E(q_t \mid I_t) = 0$. By the law of iterated expectations, $E(q_t) = 0$, thus under the null hypothesis the sample mean of q_t should be zero.

Mankiw et al. use two different versions of naive price prediction. The first one is equal to the discounted value of the infinite stream of future dividends by assuming that real dividends never change from their most recently observed value, d_{t-1}. Thus

$$p_t^o = \frac{\beta}{1 - \beta} d_{t-1}. \qquad (2.29)$$

To produce a potentially smoother naive forecast, they consider the other specification where a thirty-year moving average of dividends is capitalized:

$$p_t^o = \frac{\beta}{1 - \beta} \sum_{i=1}^{30} d_{t-i}. \qquad (2.30)$$

Since p_t^o is proportional to dividends, p_t^o/p_t is proportional to the dividend-price ratio. p_t^{*k}/p_t is the k–period excess holding return (plus one). Therefore, by choosing p_t^o in this way, MRS are testing the prediction of the theory that the dividend-price ratio cannot help predict the excess holding return.

To generate a distribution of MRS statistics under the null, Mankiw et al. choose a process for dividends which contains a unit root. Mankiw et al. apply their test to annual data on the aggregate stock market from 1871 to 1988, which is an update version of those used by Shiller [68]. The conclusion of the MRS tests is that although the constant-return present-value model is rejected, the rejection is only marginal. For most specifications, the rejection of the null hypothesis is significant only at about the five or ten percent level.

Campbell and Shiller's Cointegration Approach

Following Engle and Granger [20], a vector x_t is said to be cointegrated of order (d, b), denoted $x_t\ CI(d, b)$ if, (i) all components
of x_t are integrated of order d (stationary in dth difference) and,
(ii) there exists at least one vector $\alpha(\neq 0)$ such that $\alpha' x_t$ is integrated of order $d - b$, $b > 0$. If both p_t and d_t are integrated
of order 1, the present-value model expressed by equation (2.7)
above implies that these two variables should be cointegrated.
This can be shown by defining a variable $S_t \equiv p_t - \theta d_t$ with
$\theta = \frac{\beta}{1-\beta}$. S_t is referred to as the "spread". Substracting θd_t from
both sides of equation (2.7) and rearranging it, one can obtain

$$S_t = E\left(S_t^* \mid I_t\right), \tag{2.31}$$

with

$$S_t^* = \theta \sum_{i=1}^{\infty} \beta^i (\Delta d_{t+i})$$

and the spread can be expressed as

$$S_t = \theta E\left(\Delta p_{t+1} \mid I_t\right). \tag{2.32}$$

If p_t and d_t are cointegrated such that S_t is stationary, we can
use S_t and Δd_t (or S_t and Δp_t) as stationary variables that
summarize the bivariate history of d_t and p_t in a regression test
of the present value model. Campbell and Shiller [13] consider a
VAR representation for S_t and Δd_t (with their mean removed):

$$\begin{pmatrix} \Delta d_t \\ S_t \end{pmatrix} = \begin{pmatrix} a\left(\mathcal{L}\right) & b\left(\mathcal{L}\right) \\ c\left(\mathcal{L}\right) & d\left(\mathcal{L}\right) \end{pmatrix} \begin{pmatrix} \Delta d_{t-1} \\ S_{t-1} \end{pmatrix} + \begin{pmatrix} u_{1t} \\ u_{2t} \end{pmatrix} \tag{2.33}$$

where $E\left(u_t\right) = 0$, $\mathrm{cov}(u_t) = \Omega$, $\forall t$ with $u_t = (u_{1t}, u_{2t})'$ and the
polynomials in the lag operator $a\left(\mathcal{L}\right), b\left(\mathcal{L}\right), c\left(\mathcal{L}\right)$ and $d\left(\mathcal{L}\right)$ are
all of order k. Equation (2.33) can be stacked into a first-order

system

$$
\begin{bmatrix}
\Delta d_t \\
\cdot \\
\cdot \\
\Delta d_{t-k+1} \\
S_t \\
\cdot \\
\cdot \\
S_{t-k+1}
\end{bmatrix}
=
\begin{bmatrix}
a_1 & \cdots & a_k & b_1 & \cdots & b_k \\
1 & & & & & \\
& \cdot & & & & \\
& & 1 & & & \\
c_1 & \cdots & c_k & d_1 & \cdots & d_k \\
& & & 1 & & \\
& & & & \cdot & \\
& & & & & 1
\end{bmatrix}
\begin{bmatrix}
\Delta d_{t-1} \\
\cdot \\
\cdot \\
\Delta d_{t-k} \\
S_{t-1} \\
\cdot \\
\cdot \\
S_{t-k}
\end{bmatrix}
+
\begin{bmatrix}
u_{1t} \\
0 \\
\cdot \\
0 \\
u_{2t} \\
0 \\
\cdot \\
0
\end{bmatrix}
$$

$$(2.34)$$

where blank elements are zero. Equation (2.34) can be written as

$$z_t = A z_{t-1} + v_t. \tag{2.35}$$

For all i,

$$E\left(z_{t+i} \mid H_t\right) = A^i z_t, \tag{2.36}$$

where H_t is the limited information set containing current and lagged values of p_t and d_t or, equivalently, of z_t.

Campbell and Shiller [13] test a set of cross-equation restrictions implied by the present-value model for the VAR system. The restrictions are obtained by first projecting equation (2.31) onto the information set H_t. The left-hand side of (2.31) is unchanged, since S_t is in H_t. Equation (2.31) can be rewritten as

$$g' z_t = \theta \sum_{i=1}^{\infty} \beta^i h' A^i z_t, \tag{2.37}$$

where g' and h' are row vectors with $2k$ elements, all of which are zero except for the $(k+1)$th element of g' and the first element of h', which are unity. Under the assumption that Δd_t and S_t are stationary, if Ω is nonsingular, the following equation must hold:

$$g' = \theta \sum_{i=1}^{\infty} \beta^i h' A^i = \theta h' \beta A (I - \beta A)^{-1}. \tag{2.38}$$

A set of linear restrictions for the matrix A follows from equation (2.38): postmultiplying both sides of (2.38) by $(I - \beta A)$ gives:

$$g'(I - \beta A) = \theta h' \beta A,$$

i.e., $c_i = -\theta a_i$, $i = 1, ...k$; $d_1 = \frac{1}{\beta} - \theta b_1$; and $d_i = -\theta b_i$, $i = 2, ...k$. A Wald test statistic for equation (2.38) can be obtained for a test of the present value model.

Campbell and Shiller also use this VAR framework to conduct a volatility test. They define the "theoretical spread", S_t', as the optimal forecast, given the information set H_t, of the present value of all future changes in Δd:

$$S_t' \equiv E\left(S_t^* \mid H_t\right) = \theta h' \beta A (I - \beta A)^{-1} z_t. \qquad (2.39)$$

Since H_t is a subset of I_t, it must hold that the variance ratio

$$\mathrm{Var}\left(S_t\right) \Big/ \mathrm{Var}\left(S_t'\right) \leq 1.$$

Using data for real annual prices and dividends on the Standard and Poor composite index from 1871 to 1986, Campbell and Shiller find that the present-value model for stocks can be rejected statistically at a conventional significance level.[7] Furthermore, the point estimate of the variance ratio (67.22) is dramatically different from unity. However, the standard error is huge (86.04), thus one cannot reject the hypothesis that the variance ratio is less than or equal to unity.

Other Empirical Studies on Volatility Tests

The criticisms of early volatility tests gave proponents of market efficiency reason to hope that the apparent evidence of excess volatility was exclusively a consequence of flawed econometric procedures. The next round of volatility tests explicitly allowed for unit roots and the evidence of excess volatility became moderate. Further work on second round volatility tests includes, among others, LeRoy and Parke [48], Cochrane [15] and Durlauf and Hall [17]. In that literature the emphasis was on developing tests that have acceptable econometric properties under realistic dividend models. The evidence against the efficient market hypothesis is not so strong anymore. For example,

---

[7] The restrictions in equation (2.38) are rejected at the 7.2% level.

LeRoy and Parke [48] show that in the case where dividends follow a geometric random walk, a modified variance bound can be computed for variance of the price-dividend ratio, and that this variance bound is not violated by the data. Similar conclusions are also drawn by Cochrane [15].

2.2.3   Time-Varying Expected Returns

The autocorrelation based tests as well as the volatility tests assume a constant expected return. A natural candidate to explain the rejection of the present-value model is movements in expected returns. A general form for a model with time-varying expected returns is

$$p_t = E\left[\sum_{j=1}^{\infty} \left(\prod_{i=0}^{j} \gamma_{t+i} \right) d_{t+j} \mid I_t \right] \qquad (2.40)$$

with

$$\gamma_t \equiv E\left(\frac{p_{t+1} + d_{t+1}}{p_t} \mid I_t \right),$$

where γ_t is the expected return by the market.

As described in Section 2.2, in Lucas' consumption-based asset-pricing model the expected return depends on the ratio of the marginal utility of consumption today to that of consumption tomorrow. We can assume a plausible utility function and test for market efficiency with time-varying expected returns. One study, Campbell and Shiller [12], uses three different models for a linearized version of expected returns: the return on short debt plus a constant; the consumption-based asset-pricing model with a constant relative risk aversion, $u(c_t) = c_t^{-a}$; and the return on short debt plus a term that depends on the conditional variances of stock returns. A second study, West [79] uses equation (2.40) with expected return determined by the consumption-based asset-pricing model, also with a constant relative risk aversion where the coefficient of relative risk aversion is less than two. Neither of these two studies find that the assumed models of expected returns adequately rationalize stock price movements. Campbell and Shiller also find little plausible theoretical connection between stock prices and their measures of expected returns. It should be mentioned that both papers allow for unit roots so that there is no obvious reason to believe that a small-sample bias explains the rejection of the present value model.

Now, one could argue about the accuracy of the linearizations used, or about the validity of the models of expected returns assumed in the parametric tests in the above mentioned studies, or about how well official consumption data capture the utility flows really necessary to test the consumption-based asset pricing model. There are many nontrivial problems associated with the tests described above. But the evidence to date does not suggest that traditional models of return determination successfully explain the seemingly autocorrelated returns and excess volatility of stock prices.

The tentative conclusion that the traditional present-value models fail to explain stock price volatility suggest that a nontraditional model for return determination might be required. Excess volatility of stock prices is associated with inefficient stock markets only in the economy with a representative agent. In the artificial world researchers of excess volatility have in mind there is no trade and thus no volume data. However, technical analysis of volume data has long been a pervasive activity in security markets. Investors believe that price and volume data provide indicators of future price movements. That volume may play an important role in markets has been an important subject of empirical research.[8] In the following chapter, we will take a critical view of the consumption-based asset pricing model. Moreover, a simple asset pricing model with nontradable asset will be introduced. We will show that in an economy where agents are heterogeneous in their trading opportunity (i.e., we depart from the representative agents paradigm), excess volatility of stock prices does not imply that stock market is inefficient.

---

[8] Chapter 4 and 5 documents some of the empirical research studying stock price-volume relation.

The intuition is the following: The existence of differences in the investment opportunities induces trade. The equilibrium price will depend not only on the dividend payoff but also returns on the nontradable asset. Therefore, price volatility will be larger than that of the expected "ex-post rational prices" [equation (2.15) and (2.16)], which depends only on the variability in dividend payoff. One important feature of the model proposed is that the expectations agents have is rational expectations, which is different from the fad literature, e.g., Summers [71], Campbell and Kyle [11], who argue that trading as well as excess volatility occurs because of individuals following "irrational" trading rules.

3

The Informational Role of Volume

There is a widely held belief that price and volume data provide indicators of future price movements and that by examining these data information may be extracted on the fundamentals driving returns. If stock markets are informationally efficient in that the current price incorporates all information, we would not expect to observe any causal relationship at all between volume and stock prices. In conventional models of asset prices, such as in Lucas' consumption-based asset pricing model introduced in Chapter 2, trading volume does not play any informational role. This is justified under two paradigms: the representative agent paradigm and the rational expectations paradigm. When the asset market is complete and there exists a representative agent, asset prices are determined purely by the aggregate risk. Trading in the market only reflects the allocation of the aggregate risk and the diversification of individual risks among investors. It provides *no additional information* about prices given certain characterizations of the aggregate risk. The poor empirical performance of the representative agent model has led researchers to develop models with heterogeneous investors and incomplete asset markets.[1]

Trade between investors exists because they are different individuals. However, in a model in which all agents are rational and differ only with respect to information, volume is always zero in equilibrium. This is the well-known "no-trade theorem" (Milgrom and Stokey, [56], Varian, [76]): The no-trade theorem characterizes a class of situations in which diversely informed traders extract information from equilibrium prices so efficiently that literally no volume of trade can occur in equilibrium.

To explain volume data from financial markets, a model is needed for which the no-trade theorem fails to hold and which gives us enough flexibility to model all the dynamics observed in the data. In this chapter, we begin our analysis by introducing the Grossman-Stiglitz ([36] and [37]) model which is the standard rational expectations framework typically employed to investigate financial markets with differential information. We illustrate why in this framework volume plays no informational role. Moreover, to demonstrate that the no-trade problem is a difficult one to obviate, we investigate a model recently developed by Blume, Easley and O'Hara [6] which is intended to explain the informational role of volume. This investigation is taken from Hsu and Orosel [41]. Section 2 shows that in the model by Blume, Easley and O'Hara, in spite of agents receiving information of different quality, volume is zero in equilibrium. In Section 3 we propose an alternative model with agents differing in their investment opportunities. The model is a fully dynamic one in which all agents have rational expectations and symmetric information. This model does not suffer from the no-trade problem. Moreover, the return-volume dynamics implied by this simple model coincide with main empirical regularities documented by previous empirical work:[2] (i) time-varying volatility of stock returns; (ii) positive relation between volume

---

[1] See, among others, Campbell and Kyle [11], Wang [77] and Lucas [51].

[2] See Chapter 4 and Chapter 5 for more detailed description of empirical regularities of stock volume and return.

and the magnitude of price changes; (iii) positive relation between volatility and volume. In addition, the model predicts a non-monotonic relation between the serial correlation of stock returns and volume. This can explain the controversial findings in empirical literature studying the relation between volume and the persistence of stock returns. Finally, the model imposes restrictions on the bivariate distribution of return and volume which will be estimated and tested in Chapter 6.

3.1   Standard Grossman-Stiglitz Model

Consider a repeated economy with two kinds of assets, one risky and one riskless asset. The risky asset has a fixed total supply which, for simplicity, is assumed to be zero.[3] One share of the risky asset pays ψ units of the single consumption good at the end of each period, where ψ is a random variable. The riskless asset has infinitely elastic supply and pays one unit of the single consumption good for sure at the end of each period. There are N agents in the economy, indexed by $i = 1, 2, ...N$. Assume that the agent i has a constant absolute risk-aversion utility with coefficient of risk aversion equal to γ:

$$U\left(W_i\right) = -\exp\left(-\gamma W_i\right), \tag{3.1}$$

where W_i is the terminal wealth. Each agent begins with zero endowment of the risky asset and some exogenous endowment n_i of the riskless asset. All agents have a common probability belief under which ψ is normally distributed with $\psi \sim N\left(\psi_0, \sigma\psi^2\right)$.

Before trading takes place, agent i receives a private signal

$$y_i = \psi + \varepsilon_i, \tag{3.2}$$

where ε_i is i.i.d. and normally distributed with $E\left(\varepsilon_i\right) = 0$ and $\mathrm{Var}(\varepsilon_i) = \sigma\varepsilon^2$, $\forall i$. Additionally, ψ and $(\varepsilon_i)_{i=1}^{\infty}$ are assumed to be independent for all i.

---

[3] The important thing is that the supply is fixed over time.

In rational expectations models of the type considered here, equilibrium involves a set of price and demand functions that satisfy the following properties. First, agents conjecture the equilibrium price function given their information sets. Based on these price functions and on observation of the equilibrium price, agents determine their demand for the risky asset. In an equilibrium, these price conjectures are correct and the market clears. To construct such an equilibrium, suppose that each agent conjectures the price of the risky asset, denoted as p, to be a nonconstant affine function of aggregate information $\bar{y} \equiv \frac{1}{N} \sum_{i=1}^{N} y_i$ and is invertible. Denote the realization of the signal agent i receives as Y_i.[4] Then, conditional on the price p and the signal Y_i, ψ is normally distributed with mean and variance as follows:

$$E\left[\psi \mid y_i = Y_i, p\left(\bar{y}\right) = p\left(\overline{Y}\right)\right] \qquad (3.3)$$
$$= E\left(\psi \mid y_i = Y_i, \bar{y} = \overline{Y}\right)$$
$$= E\left(\psi \mid \bar{y} = \overline{Y}\right)$$
$$= \psi_0 + \beta\left(\overline{Y} - \psi_0\right)$$

$$\mathrm{Var}\left[\psi \mid y_i = Y_i, p\left(\bar{y}\right) = p\left(\overline{Y}\right)\right] \qquad (3.4)$$
$$= \mathrm{Var}\left(\psi \mid y_i = Y_i, \bar{y} = \overline{Y}\right)$$
$$= \mathrm{Var}\left(\psi \mid \bar{y} = \overline{Y}\right)$$
$$= (1 - \beta)\,\sigma\psi^2$$

where $\overline{Y}$ is the realization of $\bar{y}$ and $\beta = \sigma\psi^2 \big/ \left(\sigma\psi^2 + \frac{\sigma\varepsilon^2}{N}\right)$.

Normalize the price of the riskless asset to 1. If the realization of her private signal is Y_i, agent i's problem is

$$\max_{\lambda_i} E\left[-\exp\left(-W_i\right) \mid y_i = Y_i, p\left(\bar{y}\right) = p\left(\overline{Y}\right)\right] \qquad (3.5)$$

$$\text{s.t. } W_i = (\psi - p)\,\lambda_i + n_i$$

---

[4] In the following, we will use upper case letters to denote realizations of random variables.

where λ_i is the number of shares of the risky asset agent i chooses to hold. With the price of the riskless asset normalized to 1, the rate of return on the riskless asset is zero. The demand for the risky asset of agent i then is

$$
\begin{aligned}
\lambda_i &= \frac{E\left[\psi \mid y_i = Y_i, p\left(\overline{y}\right) = p\left(\overline{Y}\right)\right] - p\left(\overline{Y}\right)}{\gamma \mathrm{Var}\left[\psi \mid y_i = Y_i, p\left(\overline{y}\right) = p\left(\overline{Y}\right)\right]} \\
&= \frac{E\left(\psi \mid y_i = Y_i, \ \overline{y} = \overline{Y}\right) - p\left(\overline{Y}\right)}{\gamma \mathrm{Var}\left(\psi \mid y_i = Y_i, \ \overline{y} = \overline{Y}\right)} \\
&= \frac{E\left(\psi \mid \overline{y} = \overline{Y}\right) - p\left(\overline{Y}\right)}{\gamma \mathrm{Var}\left(\psi \mid \overline{y} = \overline{Y}\right)}
\end{aligned}
\tag{3.6}
$$

In equilibrium demand equals supply, i.e. $\sum_{i=1}^{N} \lambda_i = 0$. Therefore, given equation (3.6), the rational expectations equilibrium price for the risky asset has the linear form

$$
p\left(\overline{Y}\right) = (1 - \beta)\psi_0 + \beta\overline{Y}.
\tag{3.7}
$$

This equilibrium price has the property that private information becomes redundant. Thus, the rational equilibrium price system symmetrizes the differences in information among individuals and is, therefore, a fully revealing price system. However, as the equilibrium price system conveys information which is superior to an agent's private signal, the optimal demand depends only on the equilibrium price. Therefore, $\lambda_i = \lambda_j, \forall i, j$, so that in equilibrium it must hold that $\lambda_i = 0$ for $i = 1, ..., N$. This implies that volume is always zero in equilibrium.[5]

If volume is identically zero, it cannot provide any information about the fundamentals relating to the asset. One might argue that by introducing other sources of heterogeneity volume statistic might capture important information. To demonstrate that the problem is difficult to avoid, in the following section

---

[5] Since each individual demand is independent of the individual signal Y_i, there is a conceptual problem: how can the market aggregate individual information if individual behaviors is independent of individual information?

we analyze a model developed by Blume, Easley and O'Hara (hereafter BEO) which is intended to investigate the informational role of volume. As shown in Hsu and Orosel, the BEO model suffers from the no-trade problem as well and thus is an inadequate framework to investigate the role of volume.

3.2   The No-Trade Result of the BEO Model

In this section we describe a model developed by Blume, Easley and O'Hara which is frequently quoted in empirical work studying the relation between volume and return (among others, Gallant, Rossi and Tauchen [32] and [33]). We present one of the results in Hsu and Orosel [41] which shows that in BEO model volume is always zero in equilibrium. The intuition of the no-trade result is as follows: Since all agents are risk-averse, trade occurs only when some agents' expected profits from trade are strictly positive. Since it is assumed that all agents have identical endowments, preferences and the same prior, the aggregate profit from trade is always zero. This implies that if there were trading, there must exist some other agents whose expected profits from trade are negative.[6] However, the latter agents will not trade (if they are not forced to). Therefore, in an equilibrium the expected profits must be zero for all (rational) agents. Since agents are risk-averse, there will be no trade in an equilibrium and thus volume is zero.

The economy considered by BEO is the one with two assets (risk-free and risky one). The value of the risky asset is ψ.[7] All agents begin with identical beliefs about the payoff ψ which is (normally) distributed as $\psi \sim N\left(\psi_0, \frac{1}{\rho_0}\right)$. Each agent receives a signal on the value of the asset. There are two types of agents in the economy. They differ from each other in two aspects: First, the signals they receive have different precision: Type 1

---

[6] With identical priors agents cannot "agree to disagree" (cf. Aumann [3]).

[7] The notation of BEO is used here. For simplicity, the time index is omitted.

(informed) agent i, $i = 1, ..., N_1$, receives a signal

$$y^{1i} = \psi + \omega + e^i$$

whereas type 2 (uninformed) agent i, $i = 1, ..., N_2$, receives a signal

$$y^{2i} = \psi + \omega + \varepsilon^i$$

where ω is a common error distributed as $\omega \sim N\left(0, \frac{1}{\rho\omega}\right)$, e^i and ε^i represent an idiosyncratic error of type 1 and type 2 traders, respectively. The distribution of e^i and ε^i is $e^i \sim N\left(0, \frac{1}{\rho^1}\right)$ and $\varepsilon^i \sim N\left(0, \frac{1}{\rho^2}\right)$. BEO assume that $\rho^1 \in (\rho^2, \rho\omega)$, i.e. the signals received by type 1 agents are more precise than those received by type 2 agents. Second, ρ^1 is assumed to be unknown for type 2 traders, whereas ρ^2 (as well as all other parameters) are publicly known. All the random variables are assumed to be independent. All agents maximize their expected utility as given in (3.1). Each agent is endowed with n_0 units of the riskless asset and zero units of the risky asset.

Define $\rho^{s1} \equiv \rho\omega\rho^1 \left(\rho\omega + \rho^1\right)^{-1}$ and $\rho^{s2} \equiv \rho\omega\rho^2 \left(\rho\omega + \rho^2\right)^{-1}$. BEO assume that agents cannot use the information the current price contains when selecting their trade. According to BEO, the demand for the risky asset of type 1 agent i is

$$\rho_0 \left(\psi_0 - p\right) + \rho^{s1} \left(y^{1i} - p\right) \tag{3.8}$$

and

$$\rho_0 \left(\psi_0 - p\right) + \rho^{s2} \left(y^{2i} - p\right) \tag{3.9}$$

for type 2 agent i. This implies that the equilibrium price has the form

$$p = \frac{\rho_0\psi_0 + \mu\rho^{s1}\overline{y}^1 + (1 - \mu)\rho^{s2}\overline{y}^2}{\rho_0 + \mu\rho^{s1} + (1 - \mu)\rho^{s2}} \tag{3.10}$$

with $\mu \equiv \frac{N_1}{N_1 + N_2}$, and $\overline{y}^1$ and $\overline{y}^2$ are the mean signals of type 1 and 2 agents, respectively. In a large economy, the price is

$$p = \frac{\rho_0\psi_0 + (\mu\rho^{s1} + (1 - \mu)\rho^{s2})\theta}{\rho_0 + \mu\rho^{s1} + (1 - \mu)\rho^{s2}} \tag{3.11}$$

because the Strong Law of Large Numbers applies so that the average signals of both types converge to θ, which is defined as $\theta \equiv \psi + \omega$.

Because ρ^1 (and thus ρ^{s1}) is unknown to type 2 agents, they cannot infer the value of θ by observing price alone. Thus, BEO argue that there is a reason for type 2 agents to look at volume. In their Proposition 3 (page 172) it is shown that if $\rho^1 \in (\rho^2, \rho\omega)$ price and volume reveal θ and ρ^1. The "equilibrium price" in equation (3.11) is not fully revealing because the true value of the asset ψ cannot be inferred from price and volume. Therefore, a partial revealing equilibrium seems to be constructed by BEO in which volume statistic has important information contents.

However, as shown in Hsu and Orosel [41], Proposition 2, given the demand functions (3.8) and (3.9) in BEO model, there exists no equilibrium with positive volume and an equilibrium price which is linear in θ. The reason is that the decision on whether or not to trade would depend (only) on the realization of the signal (denoted as Y^i) an agent receives. However, the distribution of the signal over agents varies with the realization of θ. This implies that for each type the average signal of agents who would trade ($\overline{y}^1$ and $\overline{y}^2$) is not equal to θ. Furthermore, the differences between the average signals ($\overline{y}^1$ and $\overline{y}^2$) and θ are not constant. Therefore, the percentage of the agents who trade as well as the average signals are not constant. As a consequence, the price function [equation (3.11)] derived by BEO, which is linear in θ, is not market clearing. In addition, in an equilibrium in which the equilibrium price is linear in θ the percentage of both types of agents participating the trade is zero. In another words, volume is zero in such an equilibrium. The formal proof is given in the Appendix of Hsu and Orosel ([41]).

To sum up, because of no-trade theorems, *in every model in which agents are rational and differ only with respect to information, volume is always zero in equilibrium. In order to investigate the role of volume, one needs a model which includes non-informational reasons for trade in addition to differences in information.*[8] In the following section we propose a simple model of this kind.

3.3   A Model with Nontradable Asset

In his 1994 paper, Wang [77] introduced a simple, fully dynamic asset pricing model to study the relation between volume and the nature of heterogeneity among investors. In his setup, agents are heterogeneous in their investment opportunities. The model is able to explain the positive relation between volume and absolute price changes as well as positive autocorrelation of volume data, but not other empirical regularities like, for example, the positive relation between volume and stock price volatility. Part of this is due to the distributional assumption of unconditional normality of shocks in the economy. In this section, we modify Wang's model by relaxing the assumption of the shocks having constant volatility. We propose that the shocks in the economy have deterministic but time-varying volatility. Ideally, we would use a time-varying stochastic volatility. However, if the volatility is stochastic, there is no closed form solution for the intertemporal optimization problem because the form of the value function is unknown. Therefore, the analysis of the dynamics between volume and return becomes intractable. With a deterministic time-varying volatility, we show that there is a rational expectations equilibrium in which the market clearing price is linear in the returns of the risky assets in the economy.

We further show analytically that the predicted relation between the serial correlation of stock returns and volume is not monotonic: it can be positive or negative, depending on the probability structure of the shocks. This result can explain the controversial findings in empirical literature studying the relation between volume and the persistence of stock returns. The relation between volume and volatility is more complicated and

---

[8] Hsu and Orosel [41], page 8.

cannot be derived analytically. Thus, we will rely on the numerical exercises which will be reported in Chapter 4.

In Chapter 4 we present numerical evidence that this economy can mimic the stochastic volatility properties of financial returns. This suggests that the assumption of deterministic volatility might be a reasonable first approximation. In the simulations to be reported in Chapter 4, we model the deterministic volatility process by the chaotic tent map dynamics which is known to behave similar as an AR(1) process (Sakai and Tokumaru, [63]). The simulated stock return mimics the GARCH behavior quite well. Thus, as noted above, modelling the volatility as an autocorrelated time-varying deterministic process can be viewed as an approximation to the ARCH or GARCH process (Engle, [18], Bollerslev, [7]) which is one of the most prominent tools for characterizing changing variance of financial time series. The ambiguous relation between the serial correlation of stock return and volume as well as the positive relation between volume and the volatility of stock return are confirmed in a series of empirical and numerical examples. Therefore, the data generated from the simple dynamic asset pricing model with a time-varying volatility can mimic the volume-persistence and volume-volatility relation revealed in the observed data well.

In the following, we modify Wang's model by relaxing the assumption of the shocks having constant volatility. We propose that the shocks in the economy have deterministic but time-varying volatility. It is shown that there is a rational expectations equilibrium in which the market clearing price is linear in the state variables.

In the economy all agents can trade both riskless (bond) and risky (stock) assets. Bonds guarantee a gross rate of return $R \equiv 1 + r$. The supply of bonds is infinitely elastic. The dividend payoff of each share of stock is D_t in period t. The total supply of stock shares per capita is fixed and is normalized to one. There are two types of traders in the economy and differ from each other in their investment opportunities: type A traders have the opportunity to invest in a risky asset which is not available to type B traders. The (for type B traders) nontradable asset has an excess rate of return of q_t for period t whose conditional mean, conditional upon information in period $t-1$, is denoted as Z_{t-1}. The percentage of type A traders is ω and consequently the percentage of type B traders is $1-\omega$.

The dividend payoff of each share of stock in period t is assumed to follow an $AR(1)$ process:

$$D_t = a_D D_{t-1} + \epsilon_{D,t}, \tag{3.12}$$

with $0 \le a_D < 1$ and $\epsilon_{D,t} \sim i.i.d.\ N(0,\sigma_D^2)$. The excess rate of return on the (for type B traders) nontradable asset q_{t+1} for period $t+1$ is assumed to follow the process

$$q_{t+1} = Z_t + \epsilon_{q,t+1}, \quad \epsilon_{q,t} \sim i.i.d.\ N(0,\sigma_q^2), \tag{3.13}$$

$$Z_t = a_Z Z_{t-1} + \epsilon_{Z,t}, \quad \epsilon_{Z,t} \sim N(0,\sigma_{Z,t}^2),$$

with $0 \le a_Z < 1$ and $\sigma_{Z,t}^2 = f\left(\sigma_{Z,t-1}^2; t\right)$. It is assumed that the innovations $\epsilon_{D,t}$, $\epsilon_{q,t}$ and $\epsilon_{Z,t}$ are jointly normal and uncorrelated except for $\epsilon_{D,t}$ and $\epsilon_{q,t}$, whose covariance, denoted as $\sigma_{D,q}$, is strictly positive.

For all traders, preferences are assumed to be additively time separable with exponential per period utility which has constant absolute risk aversion ($CARA$). All traders maximize their expected life time utility:

$$\max E_t\left[-\sum_{s=t}^{T}\beta^{s-t}\exp(-\gamma c_s) - \beta^{T-t+1}\exp\left(-\alpha W_{T+1}\right)\right]$$

$$\text{s.t. } W_{t+1} = (W_t - c_t)R + X_t'Q_{t+1}. \tag{3.14}$$

where E_t is the expectation operator conditioned upon traders' information in period t, c_t is an agent's consumption in period t, β the discount factor and γ the risk aversion coefficient, $\alpha = \frac{r\gamma}{R}$,

[9] W_t is his wealth in period t, $\mathbf{X}_t$ is his portfolio and $\mathcal{Q}_{t+1}$ is the returns on risky assets in $t + 1$.[10]

Denote the stock price in period t as P_t. The information structure in this economy is that both types of traders observe P_t, D_t and Z_t in time t. Therefore, both types of traders have the information set $\mathfrak{I}_t = \{D_s, P_s, Z_s \mid s \leq t\}$.

Given the assumed process for Z_t we have the following result:

Proposition 1 *The economy described above has a rational expectations equilibrium in which the equilibrium stock price is*

$$P_t = p_{0,t} + aD_t - p_{Z,t}Z_t, \tag{3.15}$$

where $a = \frac{a_D}{R - a_D}$ and where $p_{0,t}$ and $p_{Z,t}$ are deterministic sequences.

Proof. See Appendix A.

Given the equilibrium price in equation (3.15), the excess return per share of the stock Q_{t+1} equals

$$\begin{aligned} Q_{t+1} &= p_{0,t+1} - Rp_{0,t} + (Rp_{Z,t} - a_Z p_{Z,t+1}) Z_t + (1 + a)\,\epsilon_{D,t+1} \\ &\quad - p_{Z,t+1}\epsilon_{Z,t+1}. \end{aligned} \tag{3.16}$$

The conditional variance of return, denoted as $\mathrm{Var}_t\,(Q_{t+1})$, equals

$$\begin{aligned} &\mathrm{Var}_t\,(Q_{t+1}) \\ &= \mathrm{Var}_t\left[(1 + a)\,\epsilon_{D,t+1} - p_{Z,t+1}\epsilon_{Z,t+1}\right] \\ &= (1 + a)^2\,\sigma_D^2 + p_{Z,t+1}^2\sigma_{Z,t+1}^2. \end{aligned}$$

Therefore, the volatility of stock return is time-varying.

The optimal stock demand of type B traders, denoted as X_t^B, equals[11]

$$X_t^B = f_{0,t}^B + f_{Z,t}^B Z_t, \tag{3.17}$$

---

[9] The particular choice for the salvage term is motivated by the analytical convenience. It allows for analytical solution of the Bellman equation.

[10] Thus, for an A type trader, $\mathbf{X}_t = (X_t, y_t)'$ where X_t is his stock shares and y_t is his investment in the nontradable asset and $\mathcal{Q}_{t+1} = (Q_{t+1}, q_{t+1})'$. For an B type traders, $\mathbf{X}_t = X_t$ and $\mathcal{Q}_{t+1} = Q_{t+1}$ since they cannot invest in the nontradable asset.

[11] See Appendix A.

where $f_{0,t}^B$ and $f_{Z,t}^B$ are functions of $\sigma_{Z,t}^2$. Trading volume in time t can be written as $1-\omega$ times the absolute changes of the optimal holding of stock from B type traders. Therefore, volume equals

$$
\begin{aligned}
V_t &= (1-\omega)\left|X_t^B - X_{t-1}^B\right| \qquad\qquad (3.18)\\
&= (1-\omega)\left|f_{0,t}^B - f_{0,t-1}^B + f_{Z,t}^B Z_t - f_{Z,t-1}^B Z_{t-1}\right|.
\end{aligned}
$$

The ambiguous relation between volume and expected return is given in the following Proposition:

Proposition 2 *Given the current excess return and volume, next period's expected excess return is*

$$
E\left(\widetilde{Q}_{t+1} \mid \widetilde{Q}_t, V_t\right) = \lambda_{0,t+1} + \lambda_{1,t+1}V_t^2 + \lambda_{2,t+1}\widetilde{Q}_t + \lambda_{3,t+1}V_t^2\widetilde{Q}_t
$$
$$
+ \; high\text{-}order \; terms. \qquad\qquad (3.19)
$$

where $\widetilde{Q}_{t+1} \equiv Q_{t+1} - p_{0,t+1} + Rp_{0,t}$, *i.e., the random part of excess return,* $\lambda_{0,t+1}, \lambda_{1,t+1}, \lambda_{2,t+1}$ *and* $\lambda_{3,t+1}$ *are functions of* $\sigma_{Z,t}^2$*. The coefficient* $\lambda_{3,t+1}$ *can be positive or negative, depending on the parameters in the economy.*

Proof. See Appendix B.

From the proposition above, the sign of $\lambda_{3,t+1}$ is ambiguous. Therefore, the economic model described above does not imply any monotonic relation between volume and the first order autocorrelation of stock return. One can further write V_t as

$$
V_t = \widetilde{V}_t + \overline{V}
$$

with $\overline{V} = E(V_t)$ is the mean volume. To the same order approximation, equation (3.19) becomes

$$
E\left(\widetilde{Q}_{t+1} \mid \widetilde{Q}_t, V_t\right) = \phi_{0,t+1} + \phi_{1,t+1}\widetilde{V}_t + \left(\phi_{2,t+1} + \phi_{3,t+1}\widetilde{V}_t\right)\widetilde{Q}_t
$$
$$
+ \; high\text{-}order \; terms. \qquad\qquad (3.20)
$$

with $\phi_{0,t+1} = \lambda_{0,t+1} + \lambda_{1,t+1}\overline{V}^2$, $\phi_{1,t+1} = 2\lambda_{1,t+1}\overline{V}$, $\phi_{2,t+1} = \lambda_{2,t+1} + \lambda_{3,t+1}\overline{V}^2$, $\phi_{3,t+1} = 2\lambda_{3,t+1}\overline{V}$. Again, since $\lambda_{3,t+1}$ can be positive or negative and $\overline{V} > 0$, the sign of $\phi_{3,t+1}$ is ambiguous.

4
Volume and Volatility of Stock Returns

There are two strands to the empirical literature on high frequency stock price and volume movement. One strand documents the positive relation between volatility of stock returns and trading volume (Tauchen and Pitts [73], Gallant, Rossi and Tauchen, [32]). The other strand focuses on the relation between volume and the serial correlation of stock returns.

There is little theoretical justification for the finding of positive association between volume and volatility. One explanation is given by Clark [14] and Tauchen and Pitts [73]: Over the day $t - 1$ to t, a random number of individual pieces of information impinge the market which triggers an independent price movement and transactions. Thus, the variance of the daily return is a random variable with a mean proportional to the mean number of daily transactions. Trading volume is positively related to the number of within-day transactions and therefore volume is related positively to the variability of returns.

As for the relation between market volume and the serial correlation in stock returns, different models predict different relation. Campbell, Grossman and Wang [10] find a negative relation and justify their finding by a theoretical model with different groups of investors interacting in the market: the demand for stock of one group of traders is exogenous and the other investors are myopic risk-averse utility maximizers. When the first group of traders' random shifts in the stock demand are accommodated by the risk averse traders, expected return on the stock changes which should be associated with an increase in trading volume. Morse [57] and Antoniewicz [2], on the other hand, find that returns are more persistent when trading volume is high. Morse [57] explains this by constructing a theoretical framework in which traders have diverse information. When traders' information is more diverse, trading volume is high. During these periods learning takes place, beliefs converge and correlations of return are induced by this convergence mechanism. Finally, LeBaron [47] finds different results when the detrending procedure of volume is different. In addition, using individual stock data Tauchen, Zhang and Liu [74] find no influence of volume on the serial correlation of stock returns.

None of the theoretical models above involves a dynamic optimization behavior of agents. In this Chapter, we ask whether the relation between volume, volatility and persistence of stock return can be deduced in the model with time-varying volatility introduced in Chapter 3. We present numerical evidence that this economy can mimic the stochastic volatility properties of financial returns. This suggests that the assumption of deterministic volatility might be a reasonable first approximation.

The relation between volume and volatility is more complicated and cannot be derived analytically. Thus, we rely on the numerical exercises. In the simulations to be reported below, we model the deterministic volatility process by the chaotic tent map dynamics which is known to behave similar as an AR(1) process (Sakai and Tokumaru, [63]). The simulated stock return mimics the GARCH behavior quite well. Thus, as noted above, modelling the volatility as an autocorrelated time-varying deterministic process can be viewed as an approximation to the ARCH or GARCH process (Engle, [18], Bollerslev, [7]) which is one of the most prominent tools for characterizing changing variance of financial time series. The ambiguous relation between the serial correlation of stock return and volume as well as the positive relation between volume and the volatility of stock return are confirmed in a series of empirical and numerical examples. Therefore, the data generated from the simple dynamic asset pricing model with a time-varying volatility can mimic the volume-persistence and volume-volatility relation revealed in the observed data well.

4.1 Empirical and Numerical Results

We now approach the question of this chapter: what is the relationship between volume, volatility and serial correlation of stock return implied by the economic model introduced in Chapter 3? We try to answer it by means of examining a number of numerical simulations and compare the results with observed data. That the serial correlation can virtually have any sign, as shown analytically in Proposition 2, Section 3.3, will be further supported by the simulated as well as the observed data. The relation between return volatility and volume cannot be derived analytically because both the coefficients in the volume equation (3.18) and conditional second moments of return are functions of the time-varying volatility of nontradable asset $\sigma_{Z,t}^2$. However, the data generated from the artificial economic world described in Chapter 3 exhibit a highly significant positive correlation between volume and the one-step ahead volatility of stock return. This significant relation is further confirmed by using observed data.

The observed data set comprises daily closing prices and the number of shares traded on the New York Stock Exchange for four heavily traded stocks: Boeing (BA), International Business Machine (IBM), Coca Cola (KO) and Minnesota Mining & Manufacturing (MMM). The sample period is from April 5, 1987 to October 14, 1996, for 3000 observations on each series. We choose individual stock data instead of index data. The plot of theses series are presented in Figure 4.1. There are two reasons for using individual data: First, in our artificial world described in Section 1 there is only one risky asset traded in the economy and volume is the net trade of this single stock. With aggregate volume data, if traders by or sell one stock in exchange for the others, the net trade of the risky asset might be overestimated. Second, the problem of nonsynchronous trading may lead to spurious positive autocorrelation in an index return.

The simulated data are obtained by calibrating the theoretical model with the risk aversion coefficient $\gamma = 1.00$ and the discount factor $\beta = 0.9995$ which implies approximately a consistent interest rate of $r = 0.05$ percent $(= 0.0005)$. The proportion of A type traders (ω) in the economy is set to equal 0.01. The autocorrelation coefficient of dividend (a_D) as well as of the expected return on the nontradable asset (a_Z) are set to be equal to 0.99. The variance of dividend (σ_D^2) and the nontradable asset (σ_q^2) are set to 1 and the covariance $(\sigma_{D,q})$ equals 0.25.

The time-varying volatility of Z_t is modelled by the chaotic tent map dynamics. The (asymmetric) tent maps have the nice property that the autocorrelation coefficients coincide exactly with the autocorrelation coefficients of an AR(1) process (Sakai and Tokumaru, [63]). Modelling volatility in this way can be considered as an approximation for a GARCH process (Bollerslev, [7]).[1] The asymmetric tent map is the continuous piecewise linear map $f_{h,[0,b]} : [0, b] \mapsto [0, b]$ defined as

$$
\begin{aligned}
f_{h,[0,b]}\left(x\right) &= \frac{2x}{1+h} & \text{if } 0 \le x \le \frac{(1+h)\,b}{2} \\
&= \frac{2\left(b-x\right)}{1-h} & \text{if } \frac{(1+h)\,b}{2} \le x \le b
\end{aligned}
$$

where $-1 < h < 1$. In our simulation, we set $h = 0.9$, i.e. the first order autocorrelation of the time-varying volatility $\sigma_{Z,t}^2$ equals 0.9, in order to mimic the persistence of the volatility on stock returns found in high frequency financial time series. The

---

[1] Using the Efficient Method of Moment, Gallant, Hsieh and Tauchen [30] shows that the result by fitting the variance with a deterministic process (a chaotic Mackey-Glass sequence) is better than a standard stochastic volatility model for daily Standard and Poor's Composite Price Index.

volatility varies between 0 and b. We set $b = 1, 10, 50$ and 100 in various settings, denoted as setting A, B, C, and D, respectively. This implies that on the average the volatility of Z_t contributes 3 percent, 19 percent, 56 percent, 74 percent of the volatility in stock return in simulation setting A, B, C, and D, respectively.[2] For all numerical examples, we simulate 1000 data set, each of which with a length of 15,000 periods. We discard the last 12,000 periods to ensure that the effect of terminal condition in the maximization problem does not distort the result. To be more precise, for $y_t = (r_t, V_t)'$ with $r_t \equiv \frac{Q_t}{P_{t-1}}$ denoting stock return per dollar, the simulated data set $\{y_t^i\}_{t=1}^T$ is generated by the structural model described in Section 1 with $T = 15,000$ and $i = 1, 2, ..., 1000$.

Figure 4.2 to 4.5 shows the scatter plots of stock return and volume series from the observed data and simulated data. The scatter plots of the observed as well as the simulated data reveal clearly a positive contemporaneous relationship between volume and the magnitude of return: days with small return tend to be days with lower than average volume, while days with large return are high volume days. As surveyed by Karpoff [42], a V-shape relation of volume to stock return has been found by virtually all empirical investigators of the return-volume relation in equity market. This consistent empirical result can be reproduced by the data generated from the model introduced in Section 3.3.

Table 4.1 and Table 4.2 report the results of relationship between volume and the first autocorrelation of stock return in the observed and simulated data, respectively. In Table 4.2, we report the proportion of the number of individual t-statistics that are less than -1.64,[3] the averaged standard errors and the centered R^2 averaged over 1000 regressions of the simulated time series. From the second column of Table 4.1, we can see that

---

[2] These pecentages are obtained from $Var_t(Q_{t+1}) = (1+a)^2 \sigma_D^2 + (p_{Z,t+1})^2 \sigma_{Z,t+1}^2$. In the numerical simulations, the maximum values of $p_{Z,t}$ for $b = 1, 10, 50$ and 100 are 16.5, 14.5, 15.3 and 16.1, respectively.
[3] This is the 5 percent level for a one-tailed test, or the 10 percent level for a two tailed test.

the first order autocorrelation of individual stock returns are not all positive as found in the value weighted average index stock returns as by, for example, Campbell et al [10]. This characteristic is exhibited in the simulated data. From the second column of Table 4.2, only 0.5, 5, 6 and 7 percent of the individual t-statistics are less than -1.64 for simulation setting A, B,C and D, respectively. The adjusted R^2s averaged over the 1000 simulated return series are less than 0.01 percent for all simulation settings.

To investigate the relation between volume and the first autocorrelation of returns, we regress one day ahead return on current return and return interacted with volume. We also regress one day ahead return on current return, current volume, return interacted with volume and squared volume, which is motivated by equation (3.20). This regression exercise is similar to that conducted in Campbell et al [10]. The analytical result predicted in Proposition 2, Section 3.3, is confirmed by the observed individual stock as well as the simulated realization: With time-varying volatility, the correlation between volume and return persistence is not always negative, as found in Campbell et al [10] or always positive, as found in Morse [57] and Antoniewics [2]. From Table 4.1, only for BA series we find a significant negative relation between volume and the autocorrelation of return. However, by putting additional term of squared volume interacted with return and/or volume, the estimate of γ_2 becomes insignificant for BA series whereas for MMM it becomes significantly positive. From Table 4.2, only 5, 6, 9 and 17 percent of the individual t-statistics of the coefficient on volume interacted with stock return are less than -1.64 for simulation setting A, B, C and D, respectively. Furthermore, the average adjusted R^2s are less than 0.01 percent for all simulation samples, which implies that the effect of trading volume on the autocorrelation of return is extremely small. By putting the additional term of volume and squared volume interacted with return, the results are not improved: only 6, 6, 9 and 12 percent of the individual t-statistics of the coefficient on volume interacted with return are less than -1.64 for simulation setting A, B, C and D, respectively. In addition, for all four simulation settings, none out of 1000 simulated series the estimated coefficients on volume and volume squared interacted with return (i.e. γ_2 and γ_3) are jointly significant different from zero at the 5% level. In short, our result supports the finding by Tauchen et al (1996), who use a nonparametric impulse response analysis and find no relation between volume and first order autocorrelation of stock return.

We now turn to the analysis of relation between volume and return volatility. The volatility of (per dollar) return can be directly obtained by

$$\sigma^2_{r,t+1} \equiv Var_t\left(r_{t+1}\right) \tag{4.1}$$

$$= Var_t\left(\frac{Q_{t+1}}{P_t}\right) = \frac{(1+a)^2 \sigma^2_D + p^2_{z,t+1}\sigma^2_{Z,t+1}}{P^2_t}.$$

The (theoretical) volatility of stock return is then regressed on simulated volume data

$$\sigma^2_{r,t+1} = c_0 + c_1 V_t + e_t, \qquad e_t \sim IID(0,\sigma^2_e). \tag{4.2}$$

In the real world the volatility is not observable. Therefore, we use the fitted value from a GARCH(1,1) model for the four individual stock returns.[4] Such a model is given by

$$r_{t+1} = \beta_0 + \beta_1 r_t + \varepsilon_{t+1} \tag{4.3}$$
$$\varepsilon_{t+1} \mid I_t \sim N\left(0, h_{t+1}\right)$$
$$h_{t+1} = a_0 + a_1\varepsilon^2_{t+1} + b_1 h_t.$$

The estimated volatility, denoted as $\widehat{h}_{t+1}$, is then regressed on volume data. The reason for doing this two-step procedure instead of putting volume as an explanatory variable directly into the volatility equation, as in Lamoureux and Lastrapes [45], is that the high correlation between contemporaneous volatility and volume causes severe problem of convergence. Since the

---

[4]Nelson (1992) shows that the volatility can be estimated very precisely from high-frequency data, even when the true model for volatility is unknown.

estimated (as well as simulated) volatilities exhibit high persistence, we regress the one step ahead volatility on the volatility and volume

$$\widehat{h}_{t+1} = \phi_0 + \phi_1 \widehat{h}_t + \phi_2 V_t. \tag{4.4}$$

For the sake of comparison, we do the same exercise for the simulated data as well.

Table 4.3 and Table 4.4 summarize our finding of positive correlation between volume and one step ahead return volatility. From Table 4.3, we can see that the regression coefficient c_1 obtained by regressing the theoretical volatilities on volume data, both of which generated from various economies, is highly significant and positive. Furthermore, from the lower panel of Table 4.4, if one approximates the volatility of stock return by estimating an GARCH(1,1) model, the estimated persistence in the (estimated) volatility, measured by $a_1 + b_1$ in equation (4.3), is very close to the calibrated value of autocorrelation in the time-varying volatility 0.9. This result can be considered as a justification to approximate a GARCH(1,1) process with the deterministic chaotic process employed in the simulation. For the volatility of all individual stock returns, the estimated ϕ_2's are positive and highly significant. This finding is consistent with results obtained in other empirical work cited in the introduction. The above reported results confirm that volume data explain much of the movement in the volatility of daily stock returns.

4.2 Summary

In this Chapter we investigated the relation between volume, first autocorrelation and volatility of stock return in a simple and fully dynamic asset pricing framework with heterogeneous agents introduced in Chapter 3. The shocks in the economy are assumed to exhibit time-varying volatility so that the volatility of the equilibrium stock price is not constant over time. Volume is endogenously generated by the intertemporal optimizing behavior of the (fully rational) agents. We simulated the model

TABLE 4.1. Volume and the first autocorrelation of return, individual stock data

$$r_{t+1} = \gamma_0 + \left(\gamma_1 + \gamma_2 V_t + \gamma_3 V_t^2\right) r_t + \gamma_4 \left(\frac{V_t}{1000}\right)$$

Sample	γ_1	γ_2	γ_3	γ_4	R^2
BA	0.033 (0.018)*				0.001
	0.077 (0.028)**	—0.021 (0.009)**			0.003
	0.130 (0.059)	—0.059 (0.044)	0.003 (0.003)		0.003
	0.128 (0.059)**	—0.059 (0.044)	0.003 (0.003)	0.124 (0.589)	0.004
IBM	—0.014 (0.018)				0.000
	—0.047 (0.042)	0.006 (0.013)			0.000
	0.026 (0.086)	—0.029 (0.047)	0.002 (0.003)		0.002
	0.028 (0.087)	—0.030 (0.047)	0.003 (0.003)	0.144 (0.391)	0.002
KO	—0.041 (0.018)**				0.002
	—0.047 (0.093)	0.001 (0.016)			0.002
	0.125 (0.153)	—0.038 (0.036)	0.001 (0.001)		0.010
	0.133 (0.160)	—0.039 (0.038)	0.001 (0.001)	0.137 (0.244)	0.011
MMM	—0.054 (0.018)**				0.003
	0.029 (0.049)	—0.042 (0.036)			0.008
	—0.271 (0.119)**	0.313 (0.147)**	—0.062 (0.024)**		0.019
	—0.277 (0.124)**	0.323 (0.156)**	—0.064 (0.026)**	—0.835 (1.106)	0.021

In the parenthesis is the heteroskedasticity-consistent standard errors.
* and ** represents significant level of ten and five percents, respectively.
R^2s are the adjusted R^2s .

by approximating time-varying volatility of stock return with a chaotic tent map, which is known to have the property that the autocorrelation coefficients coincide exactly with the autocorrelation coefficients of an AR(1) process. The theoretical model does not imply a monotonic relation between volume and the persistence of return. This result can explain the controversial finding in empirical literature studying the relation between volume and the persistence of stock returns. In the simulated data there is a significant positive relation between volume and one step ahead stock return volatility. The ambiguous volume-persistence and positive volume-volatility relation are confirmed by using four heavily traded individual stocks. Therefore, the results obtained with the highly stylized asset pricing model with a deterministic volatility can mimic well the volume-return dynamics revealed in the observed data.

TABLE 4.2. Volume and the first autocorrelation of return, simulated data

$$r_{t+1} = \gamma_0 + \left(\gamma_1 + \gamma_2 V_t + \gamma_3 V_t^2\right) r_t + \gamma_4 V_t,$$

$$\overline{\gamma}_j = \frac{1}{1000}\sum_{i=1}^{1000}\gamma_{j,i}, \; j=1,2,3,4.$$

Sample		$\overline{\gamma}_1$	$\overline{\gamma}_2$	$\overline{\gamma}_3$	$\overline{\gamma}_4$	R^2
Setting A		0.000 (0.018)				0.000
	$t < -1.64$	0.005				
		0.000 (0.003)	0.010 (0.810)			0.000
	$t < -1.64$	0.005	0.062			
		−0.002 (0.041)	0.119 (2.319)	−1.339 (2.604)		0.001
	$t < -1.64$	0.056	0.061	0.071		
		0.000 (0.041)	−0.038 2.326)	0.415 (26.656)	0.000 (0.008)	0.001
	$t < -1.64$	0.052	0.064	0.073	0.055	
Setting B		0.000 (0.018)				0.000
	$t < -1.64$	0.059				
		0.000 (0.026)	−0.005 (0.332)			0.000
	$t < -1.64$	0.051	0.070			
		0.000 (0.031)	−0.001 (0.557)	−0.037 (1.527)		0.001
	$t < -1.64$	0.043	0.070	0.045		
		0.000 (0.031)	0.013 (0.552)	−0.081 (1,491)	−0.003 (0.004)	0.002
	$t < -1.64$	0.058	0.059	0.059	0.186	
Setting C		−0.001 (0.018)				0.000
	$t < -1.64$	0.063				
		0.000 (0.028)	−0.013 (0.179)			0.001
	$t < -1.64$	0.046	0.131			
		0.000 (0.033)	−0.013 (0.355)	−0.013 (0.722)		0.001
	$t < -1.64$	0.030	0.090	0.069		
		0.003 (0.004)	−0.038 (0.361)	0.019 (0.748)	−0.002 (0.002)	0.002
	$t < -1.64$	0.033	0.093	0.070	0.425	
Setting D		−0.003 (0.018)				0.000
	$t < -1.64$	0.078				
		0.001 (0.028)	−0.027 (0.145)			0.001
	$t < -1.64$	0.052	0.178			
		0.001 (0.034)	−0.029 (0.309)	0.000 (0.544)		0.002
	$t < -1.64$	0.031	0.103	0.100		
		0.003 (0.035)	−0.029 (0.321)	−0.039	−0.001 (0.001)	0.003
	$t < -1.64$	0.028	0.119	0.104	0.431	

1. In parenthesis are the standard errors averaged over 1000 simulations.
2. $t < -1.64$ represents the percentage of the numbers of t statistics less than -1.64.
3. R^2s are the adjusted R^2s.

TABLE 4.3. Volume and the theoretical volatility
$$\sigma^2_{r,t+1} = c_0 + c_1 V_t.$$

	c_1	s.e.	$t > 1.64$	R^2
Setting A	0.000	0.004	0.044	0.000
Setting B	0.199	0.023	1.000	0.025
Setting C	0.357	0.027	1.000	0.054
Setting D	0.333	0.023	1.000	0.066

1. s.e. is the standard error of c_1 estimates averaged over 1000 simulations.
2. The column $t > 1.64$ reports the percentage of t statistics larger than 1.64.
3. R^2 is the adjusted R^2

TABLE 4.4. Volume and volatility of return

$$r_{t+1} = \beta_0 + \beta_1 r_t + \varepsilon_{t+1}, \qquad \varepsilon_{t+1} \mid I_t \sim N(0, h_{t+1})$$
$$h_{t+1} = a_0 + a_1 \varepsilon_{t+1}^2 + b_1 h_t$$
$$h_{t+1} = \phi_0 + \phi_1 h_t + \phi_2 V_t$$

Sample	a_1	b_1	ϕ_2	R^2
BA	0.215 (0.020)***	0.328 (0.040)***	0.012 (0.000)***	0.401
IBM	0.117 (0.005)***	0.849 (0.010)***	0.042 (0.003)***	0.812
KO	0.096 (0.004)***	0.851 (0.001)***	0.084 (0.009)***	0.892
MMM	0.093 (0.003)***	0.861 (0.007)***	0.058 (0.005)***	0.837
Setting A	0.006 (0.770)	0.267 (0.252)	0.000 (0.939)	0.331
Setting B	0.012 (0.885)	0.813 (0.523)	0.002 (1.000)	0.582
Setting C	0.025 (0.979)	0.845 (0.737)	0.017 (1.000)	0.737
Setting D	0.042 (1.000)	0.886 (0.984)	0.018 (1.000)	0.841

1. For the individual stock data, it is the standard error in the parenthesis and for the simulated data, it is the percentage of t statistics larger than 1.64.

2. *** represents significant level of one percent.

3. R^2s are the adjusted R^2s from regression (4.4).

Return   **Volume**

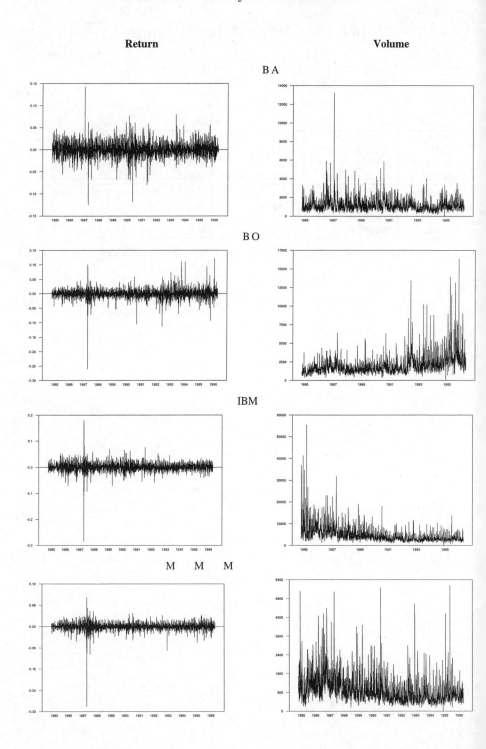

FIGURE 4.1. Return and volume series

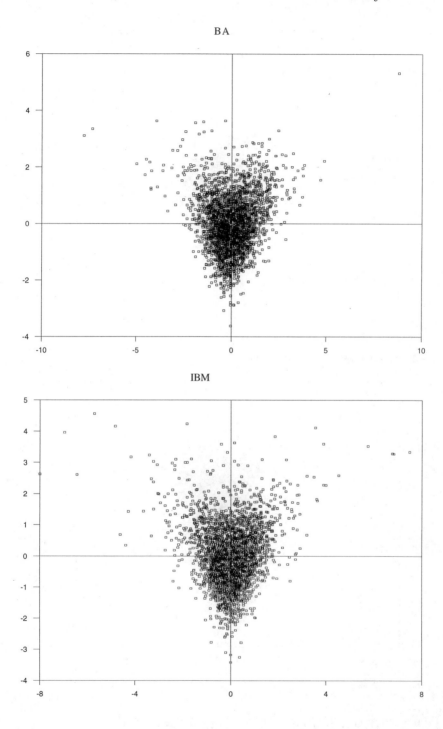

FIGURE 4.2. Scatter plot of return vs. volume

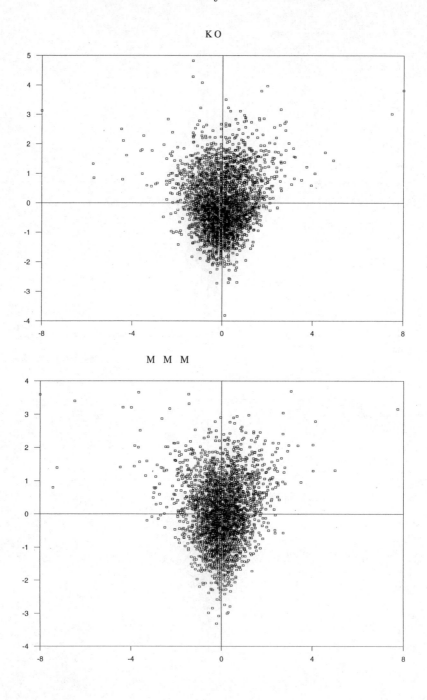

FIGURE 4.3. Scatter plot of return vs. volume

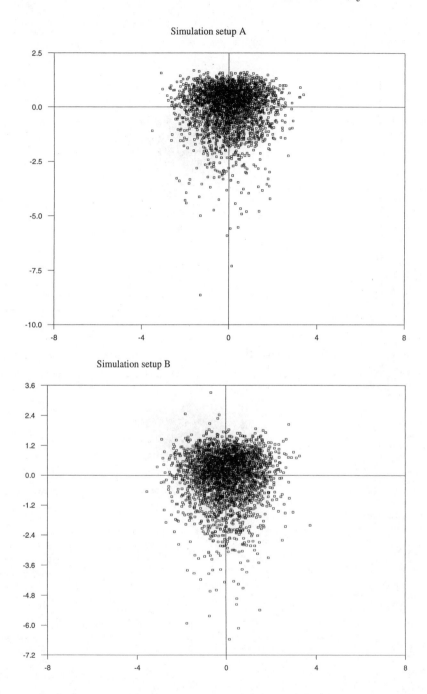

FIGURE 4.4. Scatter plot of return vs. volume

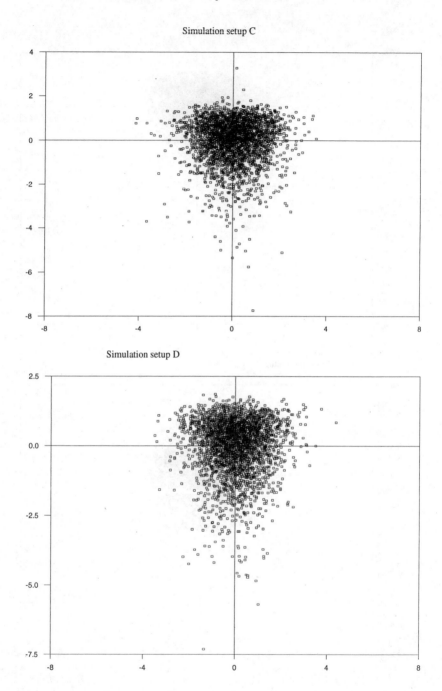

FIGURE 4.5. Scatter plot of return vs. volume

5
Nonlinear Analysis of Return and Volume

In this chapter, we undertake an empirical investigation of the joint dynamics of stock return and volume using nonparametric methods. There is substantial evidence that high frequency financial data exhibit interesting nonlinear dynamics. Among others, the empirical results of French, Schwert and Stambaugh [28], Nelson [58], [59], Baillie and DeGennaro [4], LeBaron [46] and Hsieh [40] indicate that high frequency financial data exhibit conditional heteroskedasticity and complicated patterns of higher order conditional dependence in the stock returns. By investigating nonparametrically the dynamic interrelationship between return and volume we wish to avoid bias due to a specification error, on the one hand, and provide a full set of stylized facts which a theoretical asset pricing model have to confront, on the other hand. In the following, we first apply the SNP method suggested by Gallant and Tauchen [32] to estimate the bivariate conditional density of stock return and trading volume. We then utilize the non-linear impulse response techniques developed by Gallant, Rossi and Tauchen [33] to investigate the joint dynamics of the two series.

5.1   A Preliminary Data Exploration

In this section we take a preliminary look at the data. We focus on the nonnormality of the distribution of the return and trading volume on the stock markets. The aim is to provide some motivation of choosing a semi-nonparametric approach to investigate the dynamics of stock return and volume. Since the nonparametric methods employed here are computationally expensive, we choose to use the daily Dow Jones Industrial Average and the number of shares traded daily on the New York Stock Exchange from January 1, 1952, through September 30, 1987 as the raw data set. Most of the empirical studies in return-volume relationship use this data set, which is also a reason for choosing the same data set. The Dow index series is log differenced and multiplied by 100 whereas the raw volume series is also transformed into the $\log V_t$. Since trading in the NYSE has grown steadily over time and we want to work with stationary time series, we filter the log volume data with a constant, a linear and a quadratic trend. The return series and the adjusted volume series are illustrated in Figure 5.1 and Figure 5.2, respectively.[1]

Table 5.1 gives summary statistics of the two series. In Table 5.1, *ARCH* denotes the ARCH test proposed by Engle [18] and *White* refers to the test in White [80].[2] Compared with the volume data, stock returns are more skewed to the left, and have very heavy tails. Furthermore, the autocorrelation coefficients of the return series $\rho_r(k)$ are quite low. Using the Bartlett asymptotic standard errors of $1/\sqrt{n} = 0.0011$ (with n denot-

---

[1] In many empirical studies the volume series is transformed into a turnover series. We chose not to employ this strategy for the same reason as explained in Gallant, Rossi and Tauchen [32].

[2] For both tests, the null hypothesis is

$$y = \mathbf{X}\beta + u, \qquad E(u) = 0, \qquad E(uu') = \sigma^2 \mathbf{I},$$

with $\mathbf{X}$ includes a constant term and the first lag of price changes for the price series whereas for volume series it is a constant term and the first lag of volume. For White's test, the alternative used here is $\sigma_t^2 = h(z_t'\alpha)$, where z_t includes a constant term, the lagged price changes and lagged squared price changes. For the ARCH test, the alternative is $u_t \mid \{u_s\}_{s=-\infty}^{t-1} \sim N(0, \sigma_t^2)$, where $\sigma_t^2 = b_0 + \sum_{i=1}^{7} b_i u_{t-i}^2$.

ing the number of observations), only one out of the first ten autocorrelation coefficients is statistically significant at the 1 percent level. On the contrary, the autocorrelations $\rho_{rr}(k)$ from the squared residuals of an ARMA fit are much larger. In Table 5.1, eight out of the first ten autocorrelation coefficients of the squared data are significant using the Bartlett asymptotic standard errors. This is evidence of nonlinearity.[3]

The test on general nonlinearity employed by most of the empirical work is the nonparametric test by Brock, Dechert and Scheinkman [8] which is calculated as follows. Take a data set $\{y_t; t = 1, ..., n\}$. Let $y_t^N = (y_t, y_{t+1}, ..., y_{t+N-1})$. Define

$$C\,(d, N)$$
$$= \frac{2}{n_N^2 - n_N} \left\{ \text{number of } \left(y_i^N, y_j^N \right) \text{ such that } \left| y_i^N - y_j^N \right| < d, i \neq j \right\},$$

where $n_N = n - N + 1$. The BDS statistic is

$$w(d, N) = \frac{C(d, N) - C(d, 1)^N}{\{\text{Var}\,[C(d, N) - C(d, 1)^n]\}^{1/2}}. \qquad (5.1)$$

If the process is i.i.d., $w(d, N)$ is asymptotically $N(0, 1)$ for fixed d and N. The BDS statistics in Table 5.2 show that the return series exhibits substantial nonlinearity, for $d = 0.5$, 1.0 and 2.0 times the standard error, and $N = 2, 3, ..., 10$.

The results above indicate that there might be substantial benefits from exploring a more nonparametric approach to investigate the joint dynamics of stock return and volume on the stock market. With parametric methods, there is always a risk of bias due to a specification error. In Section 2 we proceed to a conditional analysis of the data.

---

[3] According to McLeod and Li [55], the autocorrelations from squared residuals of an ARMA fit are asymptotically $N(0, 1)$. Furthermore, as noted in Granger and Anderson [35] that for a linear stationary process $corr\left(y_t^2, y_{t-k}^2 \right) = [corr\,(y_t, y_{t-k})]^2$ for all k and so departures from this would indicate nonlinearity, the autocorrelations from squared residuals are useful to identify nonlinear dependence.

TABLE 5.1. Summary statistics of return and volume, 1/1/1952 to 9/30/1987 (8987 observations)

			Test Statistics			
	Mean	s. d.	s	k	White	ARCH
return	0.02	0.88	-1.34	35.43	149.98	1189.37
					(0.00)	(0.00)
volume	0.00	0.26	0.20	0.61	5.59	610.29
					(0.20)	(0.00)

s. d. : Standard deviation; s: skewness; k: kurtosis.

	Autocorrelation Coefficients			
	return		volume	
	ρ_r	ρ_{rr}	ρ_v	ρ_{vv}
1	0.09*	0.31*	0.56*	0.20*
2	0.01	0.03*	−0.01	0.02
3	0.01	0.03*	0.10*	0.01
4	0.02	0.14*	0.06*	0.09*
5	0.01	0.06*	0.08*	0.02
6	0.01	0.01	−0.03*	0.01
7	0.01	0.05*	−0.01	0.00
8	0.00	0.04*	0.05*	0.00
9	0.01	0.04*	0.01	0.02
10	0.02	0.01	0.07*	0.05*

1. ρ_r: autocorrelations of return.

2. ρ_{rr}: autocorrelations from the squared residuals of return of an ARMA(1,1) fit.

3. ρ_v: autocorrelations of volume. ρ_{vv}: autocorrelations from the squared residuals of volume of an ARMA(6,1) fit.

4. * indicates statistical significance at the 1% level. Autocorrelation tests use the Bartlett asymptotic standard errors.

TABLE 5.2. BDS statistics of stock return

N	$d = 0.5$	$d = 1$	$d = 2$
2	18.03*	18.97*	19.15*
3	23.28*	23.58*	23.30*
4	27.47*	26.79*	25.59*
5	32.33*	29.99*	27.41*
6	38.68*	33.98*	29.28*
7	46.97*	38.30*	30.52*
8	56.94*	43.41*	31.76*
9	71.28*	49.39*	33.02*
10	92.42*	56.42*	34.34*

* indicates statistically significant at the 1% level.

FIGURE 5.1. Return series

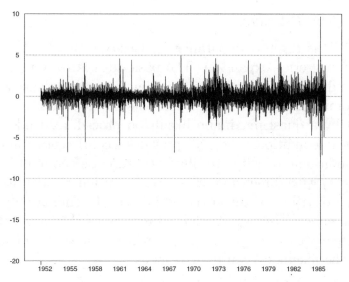

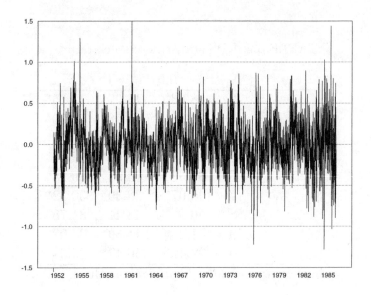

FIGURE 5.2. Adjusted volume series

5.2   Estimation of the Conditional Density

5.2.1   SNP Estimator

The SNP is a semi-nonparametric density estimator based on
a Hermite series expansion. The basic idea is to approximate
the conditional density by multiplying a normal density by a
polynomial expansion. The coefficients of the series are determined by a quasi maximum likelihood procedure. Under mild
regularity conditions, the SNP provides a consistent estimate of
the conditional density. To illustrate, suppose the multivariate
process y_t with dimension M is strictly stationary with its conditional distribution given the entire past depending only on a
finite number L of lagged values of y_t. Denote the lagged values
by $x_{t-1} = (y'_{t-L}, y'_{t-L+1,}, ..., y'_{t-1})'$, which is a vector of length
ML. The likelihood can be written as

$$\prod_{t=1}^{n} f(y_t|x_{t-1}) \int f(y, x_0)\, dy$$

with $f(y_t|x_{t-1}) = \frac{f(y_t, x_{t-1})}{\int f(y, x_{t-1}) dy}$. Given the past of y_t, one can obtain the maximum likelihood estimate of the conditional density and knowledge of the joint density $f(y_t, x_{t-1})$ is not required.

The method first proposed by Gallant and Nychka [31] approximates $f(y|x)$ by a truncated Hermite series expansion. The truncated expansion is the semi-nonparametric model. It replaces f in the likelihood and its parameters are estimated by maximizing the resulting (quasi) likelihood. The conditional density $f(y|x)$ can be consistently estimated if the number of terms in the expansion is an increasing function of the sample size. A modified Hermite expansion has the form

$$h(y|x, \theta) \propto [P(z, x)]^2 \phi(y; \mu, RR'), \qquad (5.2)$$

where $P(z, x)$ is a polynomial of degree K, $\phi(y; \mu, RR')$ denotes the M dimensional Gaussian density with mean μ and variance-covariance matrix $RR' = \Sigma$ with R a lower triangular matrix, and z is the centered and scaled random variable corresponding to y_t with

$$z = R^{-1}(y - \mu). \qquad (5.3)$$

The VAR nature of the leading term of the Hermite expansion is specified such that the location parameter of y_t is a linear function of the past:

$$\mu = a_0 + A x_{t-1}$$

where a_0 is a M by 1 and A is a M by ML coefficient matrices. The variance-covariance matrix Σ is specified in such a way that R is a linear function of absolute values of the elements of x_{t-1}:

$$\text{vech}(R) = b_0 + B|x_{t-1} - E(x_{t-1} | x_{t-2}, x_{t-3}, ..)|, \qquad (5.4)$$

where b_0 is a $(M+1)$ by 1, B is a $(M+1)ML$ dimensional coefficient matrix and "vech" is an operator which transforms an $M \times M$ matrix into an $(M+1)M/2$ vector by vertically

stacking those elements on or below the principal diagonal.[4]
The constant of proportionality is

$$\frac{1}{\int \left[p\left(z,x\right)\right]^{2} \phi\left(s\right) ds}.$$

While the classical ARCH by Engle [18] has the variance-covariance matrix of y_t depending on squared lagged residuals, the conditional heteroskedasticity suggested by SNP is more akin to that of Nelson's [59] EGARCH model.

The multivariate polynomial $P\left(z,x\right)$ with degree K_z has the form

$$P\left(z,x\right) = \sum_{|\alpha|=0}^{K_z} \left(\sum_{|\beta|=0}^{K_x} a_{\alpha\beta} x\beta \right) z\alpha \qquad (5.5)$$

where $\alpha = \left(\alpha_1, \alpha_2, ..., \alpha_M\right)'$ and $\beta = \left(\beta_1, \beta_2, ..., \beta_{ML}\right)'$ are multi-indices (vectors with integer elements), and

$$|\alpha| = \sum_{i=1}^{M} |\alpha_i|, \qquad |\beta| = \sum_{i=1}^{ML} |\beta_i|,$$

$$z\alpha = \prod_{i=1}^{M} \left(z_i\right)^{\alpha_i}, \qquad x\beta = \prod_{i=1}^{ML} \left(x_i\right)^{\beta_i}.$$

For example, in our application y_t is the bivariate process of return and volume. Suppose $x_t = y_t$, then

$$P\left(z,x\right) = \left[\sum_{i=0}^{K_z} \sum_{j=0}^{K_z} a_{ij} z_{(1)}^{i} z_{(2)}^{j} \right], \qquad (5.6)$$

with

$$a_{ij} = \left[\sum_{l=1}^{K_x} \sum_{k=1}^{K_x} a_{ijkl} x_{(1)}^{l} x_{(2)}^{k} \right], \qquad (5.7)$$

---

[4]For example,

$$\text{vech} \begin{bmatrix} R_{11} & 0 \\ R_{21} & R_{22} \end{bmatrix} = \begin{bmatrix} R_{11} \\ R_{21} \\ R_{22} \end{bmatrix}.$$

where $x_{(1)}$ and $x_{(2)}$ is the first and second element of x, respectively. The effects of K_z and K_x are such that K_z controls the shape of the conditional density departing from a VAR-ARCH with Gaussian innovations and K_x controls conditional heterogeneities. If $K_z = K_x = 0$, then $h(y|x)$ is a VAR-ARCH with Gaussian innovations. If $K_z > 0$ and $K_x = 0$, $h(y|x)$ is a VAR-ARCH and the innovations are non-Gaussian. If $K_z > 0$ and $K_x > 0$ the coefficients of the polynomial part of $h(y|x)$ depend on the past. This permits nonlinear dependence on the past and any smooth conditional density can be approximated arbitrarily accurately by making K_z and K_x large enough. Thus, any kind of skewness or kurtosis is permitted. What is ruled out are violently oscillatory density functions.

To be parsimonious, the SNP employed here distinguishes between the total number of lags under consideration, denoted by L, the number of lags in the x part of the polynomial $P(z, x)$, denoted by L_p, the number of lags in the VAR part (μ), which is L_u and the number of lags in Σ, which is L_r. Furthermore, since large values of M can generate a large number of interactions in the polynomial, there are two additional tuning parameters, I_z and I_x ,to represent suppression of these high order interactions. A positive I_z means that all interactions of order exceeding $K_z - I_z$ are suppressed; analogously, this applies to $K_x - I_x$.

The maximum likelihood estimator then is

$$\widehat{\theta}_n = \arg\max \theta \frac{1}{n} \sum_{t=1}^{n} \ln \left[h\left(y_t | x_{t-1}, \theta \right) \right]. \tag{5.8}$$

where θ consists of all the elements of a_0, A, b_0, B and α_{ijkl} $(i,\ j = 1, \dots, K_z, \ k,\ l = 1, \dots, K_x)$.

5.2.2 SNP Fitting of the Bivariate Return-Volume Conditional Density

To determine an appropriate SNP specification, we follow the same model expansion strategy as in Tauchen et al [74]. This procedure is straightforward. First, the Schwarz criterion (Schwarz [66]) is used to move along an upward expansion path until an adequate model is determined. This model is then subject to a battery of diagnostics on the conditional mean and variance.

The Schwarz criterion is

$$s_n(\widehat{\theta}) + \frac{1}{2}(p\theta/n)\log(n)$$

with small values of the criterion preferred, where

$$s_n(\widehat{\theta}) = -\frac{1}{n}\sum_{t=1}^{n}\ln\left[h\left(y_t|x_{t-1},\widehat{\theta}\right)\right]$$

is the SNP optimization criterion and $p\theta$ is the number of free parameters in the SNP model. This criterion rewards good fits as represented by a small value of s_n but uses the term $\frac{1}{2}(p\theta/n)\log(n)$ to penalize good fits gotten by means of excessively rich parametrizations. This criterion is conservative in that it selects sparser parametrizations than the Akaike information criterion (Akaike [1]), which uses the penalty term $(p\theta/n)$.[5] Between these two extremes lies the Hannan-Quinn (Hannan [38]) criterion

$$s_n(\widehat{\theta}) + (p\theta/n)\log[\log(n)].$$

The diagnostic on conditional mean is a regression of each of the standardized residuals

$$\widehat{z}_t = \text{diag}[\widehat{\Sigma}_{t-1}(y_t)]^{-1/2}[y_t - \widehat{\mu}_{t-1}(y_t)]$$

on a constant and $\{y_{t-k}, y_{t-k}\otimes y_{t-k}, y_{t-k}\otimes y_{t-k}\otimes y_{t-k}\}_{k=1}^{5}$, where $\text{diag}\left[\widehat{\Sigma}_{t-1}(y_t)\right]$ is the diagonal elements from the estimated conditional variance and $\widehat{\mu}_{t-1}(y_t)$ is the estimated conditional mean, both of which conditional on x_{t-1}. The diagnostic on the conditional variance is taken from the same regression, except that the dependent variable is the squared standardized residuals. This provides power against general nonlinear misspecification

---

[5] The Akaike criterion (Akaike [1]) does not work well here according to my own experience and personal communications with George Tauchen, because it always chooses the largest model in the present application.

of either the conditional mean or the conditional variance function.

For our data set, the estimation results are presented in Table 5.3. From Table 5.3, the initial candidate model selected by the Schwarz and by the Hannan-Quinn criterion is $L_u = 6$, $L_r = 17$, $L_p = 0$, $K_z = 9$, $K_x = 0$, $I_z = 2$ and $L_u = 5$, $L_r = 17$, $L_p = 1$, $K_z = 9$, $K_x = 1$, $I_z = 2$, respectively. However, the adjusted R^2's from the diagnostic regressions indicate that the first model leaves predictability in the squared residuals in returns and in residuals in the volume. The model preferred by Hannan-Quinn criterion does better on the diagnostics, but the adjusted R^2 of the residuals in the volume series is still larger than 1 percent. Further expansion to $L_u = 5, L_r = 17, L_p = 1, K_z = 9, K_x = 2, I_z = 2, I_x = 1$ provides us with a model in which all of the adjusted R^2's are less than 1 percent. Thus, we take this model as the preferred model characterizing the bivariate dynamic structure of daily stocj returns and volume and it will serve as the primary model for the subsequent impulse response analysis. This primary model is large, with $p\theta = 258$, and has typical features of high frequency financial data: the lag-length in the ARCH part $(L_r = 17)$ is much longer than that in the VAR part $(L_u = 5)$. Furthermore, it has a rich non-Gaussian, nonlinear structure characterized by a ninth-degree polynomial in $z_t \in R^2$ and the coefficients of the polynomial depend upon a linear function of one lag of the bivariate process.

TABLE 5.3. SNP estimations of bivariate price-volume conditional density

L_U	L_R	L_P	K_Z	I_Z	K_X	I_X	$p\theta$	$s_n\left(\widehat{\theta}\right)$	$H-Q$	BIC
0	0	0	0	0	0	0	5	283.325	283.448	283.578
1	1	0	0	0	0	0	11	236.742	237.012	237.299
1	2	0	0	0	0	0	13	234.426	234.745	235.084
1	3	0	0	0	0	0	15	232.266	232.635	233.026
1	4	0	0	0	0	0	17	230.484	230.902	231.345
1	5	0	0	0	0	0	17	230.484	230.902	230.476
1	6	0	0	0	0	0	21	228.711	229.227	229.774
1	7	0	0	0	0	0	23	228.383	228.948	229.547
1	8	0	0	0	0	0	25	227.877	228.492	229.143
1	9	0	0	0	0	0	27	227.106	227.770	228.474
1	10	0	0	0	0	0	29	226.649	227.362	228.118
1	11	0	0	0	0	0	31	226.334	227.096	227.904
1	12	0	0	0	0	0	33	226.315	227.126	227.986
2	11	0	0	0	0	0	35	224.839	225.699	226.611
2	12	0	0	0	0	0	37	224.812	225.722	226.686
2	13	0	0	0	0	0	39	224.361	225.320	226.337
2	14	0	0	0	0	0	41	224.125	225.133	226.201
2	15	0	0	0	0	0	43	223.708	224.765	225.886
2	16	0	0	0	0	0	45	223.591	224.697	225.870
2	18	0	0	0	0	0	47	223.286	224.441	225.666
2	19	0	0	0	0	0	49	223.145	224.349	225.627
3	8	0	0	0	0	0	33	224.197	225.008	225.869
3	9	0	0	0	0	0	35	223.524	224.384	225.297
3	10	0	0	0	0	0	37	223.046	223.956	224.920
4	8	0	0	0	0	0	37	222.692	223.602	224.566
4	9	0	0	0	0	0	39	222.047	223.006	224.023
4	10	0	0	0	0	0	41	221.655	222.663	223.732
4	11	0	0	0	0	0	43	221.259	222.316	223.437
4	12	0	0	0	0	0	45	221.228	222.335	223.508
4	13	0	0	0	0	0	47	220.779	221.935	223.160
4	14	0	0	0	0	0	49	220.599	221.804	223.081
4	15	0	0	0	0	0	51	220.174	221.428	222.758
4	16	0	1	0	0	0	55	219.644	220.996	222.726
4	17	0	0	0	0	0	55	219.710	221.062	222.490
4	18	0	0	0	0	0	57	219.603	221.004	222.491

	L_U	L_R	L_P	K_Z	I_Z	K_X	I_X	$p\theta$	$s_n\left(\widehat{\theta}\right)$	$H-Q$	BIC
	4	17	0	1	0	0	0	57	219.292	220.693	222.179
	4	17	0	2	1	0	0	59	219.228	220.679	222.217
	4	17	0	3	2	0	0	61	218.239	219.739	221.329
	4	17	0	4	3	0	0	63	213.465	215.014	216.665
	4	17	0	5	4	0	0	65	213.368	214.966	216.666
	4	17	0	6	5	0	0	67	212.864	214.511	216.258
	4	17	0	7	6	0	0	69	212.516	214.212	216.011
	4	17	0	8	7	0	0	71	211.983	213.728	215.579
	4	17	0	9	8	0	0	73	211.537	213.332	215.235
	4	17	0	9	7	0	0	74	211.521	213.340	215.269
	4	17	0	9	6	0	0	76	210.142	212.011	213.992
	4	17	0	9	5	0	0	79	209.333	211.275	213.335
	4	17	0	9	4	0	0	83	209.018	211.058	213.223
	4	17	0	9	3	0	0	88	208.941	211.104	213.398
	4	17	0	9	2	0	0	94	208.359	210.670	213.124
	4	17	0	9	1	0	0	101	208.292	210.775	213.409
	4	17	1	9	2	1	0	174	205.252	209.529	214.067
	4	17	1	9	2	2	1	254	203.396	209.640	216.264
	5	17	0	9	2	0	0	98	207.659	210.068	212.623
bic	6	17	0	9	2	0	0	102	207.431	209.938	212.598
h-q	5	17	1	9	2	1	0	178	205.850	208.575	213.217
	6	17	1	9	2	1	0	182	204.162	208.636	213.382
	5	17	1	9	2	2	1	258	203.355	209.698	216.426
	4	17	1	9	2	2	0	294	203.070	210.297	217.964
	5	17	1	9	2	2	0	298	202.571	209.897	217.668
	6	17	1	9	2	2	0	302	202.173	209.598	217.474

Diagnostics[6]

							Mean		Variance	
L_U	L_R	L_P	K_Z	I_Z	K_X	I_X	return	volume	return	volume
5	17	0	9	2	0	0	.0111	.0227	.0162	.0073
6	17	0	9	2	0	0	.0105	.0222	.0155	.0072
5	17	1	9	2	1	0	.0062	.0110	.0058	.0110
5	17	1	9	2	2	1	.0054	.0083	.0063	.0083

---

[6] Adjusted R^2 from the regressions of the standarized residuals on five lags of each variable. See text. "Mean" is the regression of each of the standardized residuals on a constant and $\{y_{t-k}, y_{t-k}\otimes y_{t-k}, y_{t-k}\otimes y_{t-k}\otimes y_{t-k}\}_{k=1}^{5}$ and "Variance" is the regression of each of the squared standard residuals on the same regressors.

5.3   Nonlinear Impulse Response Analysis

In this section we will perform a nonlinear impulse-response analysis to investigate the interrelationships between returns and trading volume. We follow the strategy proposed by Gallant, Rossi and Tauchen [33] which consists of computing response profiles for the conditional mean and conditional variance.

5.3.1   Conditional Mean and Conditional Variance Profile

For a linear process with homogeneous errors, the impulse response analysis (Sims, [70], Doan, Litterman and Sims, [16]) explores the dynamics of the process by investigating the effects of small movements in the innovations or linear combinations of the innovations. To illustrate, suppose

$$\Phi(\mathcal{L})y_t = \varepsilon_t \tag{5.9}$$

where

$$\Phi(\mathcal{L}) = I - \Phi_1\mathcal{L} - \Phi_2\mathcal{L}^2 - \dots - \Phi_p\mathcal{L}^p \tag{5.10}$$

indicates an $M \times M$ matrix polynomial in the lag operator $\mathcal{L}$, ε_t is a vector generalization of white noise:

$$E(\varepsilon_t) = 0$$

$$\begin{aligned} E(\varepsilon_t \varepsilon\tau') &= \Omega \quad \text{for } t = \tau \\ &= 0 \quad \text{otherwise,} \end{aligned} \tag{5.11}$$

with Ω an $M \times M$ symmetric positive definite matrix. Suppose also that $\Phi(\mathcal{L})$ is invertible so that y_t can be written in vector $MA(\infty)$ form as

$$\begin{aligned} y_t &= \Psi(\mathcal{L})\varepsilon_t \\ &= \varepsilon_t + \Psi_1\varepsilon_{t-1} + \Psi_2\varepsilon_{t-2} + \dots. \end{aligned} \tag{5.12}$$

with $\Psi(\mathcal{L}) = [\Phi(\mathcal{L})]^{-1}$. Thus, the matrix Ψ_s has the interpretation

$$\frac{\partial y_{t+s}}{\partial \varepsilon_t'} = \Psi_s. \tag{5.13}$$

Thus, the row i, column j element of Ψ_s, denoted as ψ_{ijs}, identifies the consequences of a one-unit increase in the jth variable's innovation at date t (ε_t) for the value of the ith variable at time $t + s$ (y_{t+s}), holding all other innovations at all dates constant. The sequence $\{\psi_{ijs}\}_{s=0}^{\infty}$ is then the *impulse response* of the ith variable to a one-unit positive movement in the jth variable's innovation.

For nonlinear models, it seems less useful to think in terms of an innovation. Instead, we can take certain perturbations of the conditioning arguments in conditional density function as the "shocks". The dynamics of the process can be studied by computing multi-step ahead conditional expectations of the first and second moments with respect to the perturbations. As described in Gallant, Rossi and Tauchen [33], the conditional moment profile of a strictly stationary process $\{y_t\}_{j=0}^{\infty}$ is the multistep ahead forecast of the conditional moment. Assume that the conditional distribution of the process given the entire past depends only on a finite number L of lagged values of y_t. Denote the one-step ahead conditional density of y_t as $f(y_{t+1}|x_t)$ with $x_t = (y_{t+1-L}', y_{t+2-L,}', ..., y_t')'$. Then the J-step base line conditional mean profile given initial condition $x_0 = (y_{1-L}', y_{2-L,}', ..., y_0')'$ is

$$\widehat{y}_j(x_0) = E(y_{t+j}|x_t = x_0) \qquad (5.14)$$

for $j = 1, ..., J$. If x_0 is changed by x^+ or x^- with

$$x^+ = x_0 + (0, 0, ..., \delta_y^+)',$$

$$x^- = x_0 + (0, 0, ..., \delta_y^-)',$$

for some reasonable value δ_y^+ and δ_y^- in the arguments of the conditional density, the J-step conditional mean profile conditional on x^+ or x^- is

$$\widehat{y}_j(x^+) = E(y_{t+j}|x_t = x^+),$$

and

$$\widehat{y}_j(x^-) = E(y_{t+j}|x_t = x^-),$$

for $j = 1, ...J$, respectively. Accordingly, the positive and negative impulse response of the J-step conditional mean are

$$\left\{ \widehat{y}_j \left(x^+ \right) - \widehat{y}_j \left(x_0 \right) \right\}_{j=1}^{J}$$

and

$$\left\{ \widehat{y}_j \left(x^- \right) - \widehat{y}_j \left(x_0 \right) \right\}_{j=1}^{J},$$

respectively. These response profiles provide a natural measurement to study the effect of positive (δ_y^+) and negative shocks (δ_y^-) on the conditional mean of the process.

Analogously to the conditional mean, we can measure the effects of shocks on the conditional variance by perturbing the conditional arguments. The base line profile for conditional variance is

$$\widehat{V}_j \left(x_0 \right) = \mathrm{Var} \left(y_{t+j} | x_t = x_0 \right)$$

$$= E \left\{ \left[y_{t+j} - E \left(y_{t+j} | x_t = x_0 \right) \right] \left[y_{t+j} - E \left(y_{t+j} | x_t = x_0 \right) \right]' \mid x_t = x_0 \right\}$$

for $j = 1, ...J$. Similarly, the J-step impulse responses of conditional variance to shocks δ_y^+ and δ_y^- are

$$\left\{ \widehat{V}_j \left(x^+ \right) - \widehat{V}_j \left(x_0 \right) \right\}_{j=1}^{J}, \quad \widehat{V}_j \left(x^+ \right) = \mathrm{Var} \left(y_{t+j} | x_t = x^+ \right);$$

$$\left\{ \widehat{V}_j \left(x^- \right) - \widehat{V}_j \left(x_0 \right) \right\}_{j=1}^{J}, \quad \widehat{V}_j \left(x^- \right) = \mathrm{Var} \left(y_{t+j} | x_t = x^- \right),$$

respectively, which represent the net effects of perturbations on volatility.

5.3.2   Computation

Since in general the analytical solution of the integrals of a conditional moment profile is intractable, Gallant et al [33] suggest using the Monte Carlo integration to evaluate the impulse response. First, one simulates R realizations of the process starting from $x_0 = x$: $\{y_t^r\}_{j=1}^{N}$, $r = 1, ...R$ with a large N. So y_1^r is a random drawing from $f(y|x)$ with $x = (y_{1-L}', y_{2-L}', ..., y_0')'$; y_2^r is a random drawing from $f(y|x)$ with $x = (y'_{2-L},\ldots, y'_0, y'_1)'$ and so forth. Then, for any time invariant function of a stretch of the process of length $J+1$, $g(y_{t-J}, y_{t-J+1}, \ldots, y_t)$, the conditional expectation is

$$
\begin{aligned}
\widehat{g}_j(x) &= E\left[g(y_{t+j-J}, y_{t+j-J+1}, \ldots, y_{t+j})|x_t = x\right] \\
&= \int \cdots \int g(y_{j-J}, y_{j-J+1}, \ldots, y_j) \left[\prod_{i=0}^{j-1} f(y_{i+1} \mid y_{i-L}, \ldots, y_i)\right] dy_1 \ldots dy_j \\
&\doteq \frac{1}{R} \sum_{r=1}^{R} g(y_{j-J}^r, y_{j-J+1}^r, \ldots, y_j^r).
\end{aligned}
$$

$$(5.15)$$

In our analysis,

$$
g(y_{t-L+j}, y_{t-L+j+1}, \ldots, y_{t+j}) = E\left(y_{t+j}|x_{t+j}\right) \qquad (5.16)
$$

for the conditional mean and

$$
g(y_{t-L+j}, y_{t-L++j+1}, \ldots, y_{t+j}) = \mathrm{Var}\left(y_{t+j}|x_{t+j}\right) \qquad (5.17)
$$

for the conditional variance. Under mild regularity conditions on f, the approximation error tends to zero almost surely as $R \to \infty$.[7]

5.3.3   Empirical Results

We now assess the impulse responses of the conditional mean and conditional variance of return and volume to different shocks. We apply the method of Gallant, Rossi and Tauchen [33] described above to generate empirical evidence on the multi-step ahead return and volume dynamics. The results are obtained from the SNP fit to the bivariate series $y_t = (Q_t, V_t)$ with Q_t and V_t the log daily return and adjusted volume series, respectively.

Since there can be nonlinear contemporaneous relations among variables that need to be taken into account, it can be misleading to perturb one of the variables while leaving the others fixed.

---

[7] The accuracy increases with the square root of R.

For example, as mentioned above, the volume is found to be contemporaneously related to the magnitude of the return movement. In other words, a large movement in volume is positively related to $[Q_t - E_{t-1}(Q_t)]^2$. There is a relationship between the level of the volume series and the variability of return. Since the orthogonalization strategy considers only first-moment properties, no strategy based on using orthogonalized shocks can take this relationship into account. Gallant et al [33] propose eschewing notions of orthogonalization and thinking in terms of the system's response to certain typical shocks. The scatter plot of (Q_t, V_t) is used to define shocks affecting return and volume that are consistent with the historical range of the data. The scatter plot of the data in Figure 5.3 reveals clearly the contemporaneous relationship between volume and the magnitude of return: days with small return tend to be days with lower than average volume, while days with large returns are high volume days. The scatter plot suggests the following three types of shocks as typical of the variation of the data:

A shocks:

$$\delta y_{A_1}^+ = 2.00 s_Q \qquad \delta y_{A_2}^+ = 0.00$$

$$\delta y_{A_1}^- = -2.00 s_Q \qquad \delta y_{A_2}^- = 0.00$$

B shocks:

$$\delta y_{B_1}^+ = 0.00 \qquad \delta y_{B_2}^+ = 2.00 s_V$$

$$\delta y_{B_1}^- = 0.00 \qquad \delta y_{B_2}^- = -2.00 s_V$$

C shocks:

$$\delta y_{C_1}^+ = 2.00 s_Q \qquad \delta y_{C_2}^+ = 2.00 s_V$$

$$\delta y_{C_1}^- = -2.00 s_Q \qquad \delta y_{C_2}^- = 2.00 s_V$$

where s_Q and s_V are the sample standard deviation of the return and adjusted volume series, respectively.

In this design, the A shocks are pure return shocks of ± 2.0 standard deviations with volume pinned at its mean. B shocks are pure volume shocks of ±2.0 standard deviations with no return movements. Finally, C shocks represent return movements of ±2.0 standard deviations with a volume increase equal to two standard deviations. An inspection of the scatter plot suggests that these shocks do indeed occur in the data set.

The theoretical model described in Chapter 3 can be used to interpret the design of the shock experiments. In the model, changes in the expected return of the nontradable asset results in a contemporaneous return movement and higher than normal volume. The C shocks are designed to capture this situation. In certain situations, return movements reflect arrivals of informations about the movements in the dividend payoff, which is represented by an A shock. In this case, we expect an average volume movement. The positive B shock represents the situation where expected returns on the stock as well as on the nontradable asset increase (decrease). The two effects on return offset each other, changes of the expected return on the nontradable asset would, however, be reflected in the high volume movements. The negative B shock is included for symmetry.

Figures 5.4 to 5.15 show the impulse responses of return and volume to A, B, and C shocks. As shown in Figure 5.4 and 5.5, the reaction pattern of mean responses of return to pure contemporaneous return movements without an accompanying contemporaneous volume movement (A shocks) is symmetric about the baseline and heavily dampened. Interestingly, the mean responses of volume to pure return shocks are asymmetric: volume shows a sharp rise one day after a positive return movement while a negative return shock has no effect on volume. This finding is in contrast with that of Gallant et al [33] who find a long-term slowly dampened negative response of volume to return shocks for the S&P Composite Index.

Figure 5.7 shows the volatility responses to pure return shocks. The responses of return volatility indicate that the effects of the return shocks on volatility are exceedingly slowly dampened relative to the baseline, which is very close to I-GARCH behavior found by many empirical analyses of high-frequency financial data. Furthermore, the asymmetric response pattern documented in Gallant et al [33] and Tauchen et al [74] are not found here. The responses of volume volatility are a very short-term phenomenon.

Figures 5.8 to 5.11 show the responses of the two series to a pure volume movement. It provides a clear picture that returns show hardly any response to pure volume shocks. This lack of feedback from volume to returns is consistent with the findings of Gallant et al [33] and Schwert [67].

Finally, Figure 5.12 to 5.15 provide the responses of return and volume to "nontradable asset shocks". From the figures, a positive contemporaneous return and volume movement which represents a positive shock on the expected return of the non-tradable asset has in the very short run (one day) a slightly higher impact on return and volume. The impact on volatility of both return and volume, however, is symmetric.

To sum up, three main characteristics of stock return and volume dynamics are revealed: First, return movements caused by dividend shocks (pure return shocks) have only a mild and short-term impact on subsequent movements of volume. Second, the volatility response of return to dividend shocks as well as return shocks of the nontradable asset. Third, the asymmetric response patter of the return volatility (the leverage effect) found in early literature is not confirmed by our data set.

FIGURE 5.3. Scatter plot of stock return and volume

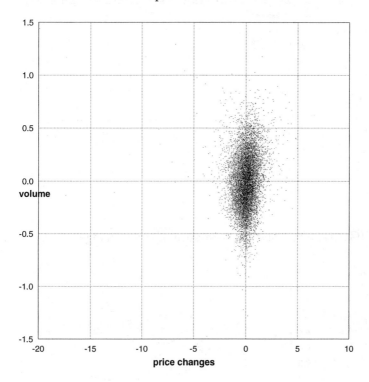

FIGURE 5.4. Mean response of price changes to A shocks

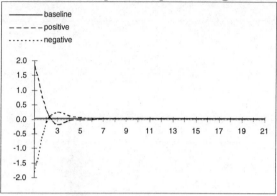

FIGURE 5.5. Volatility response of price changes to A shocks

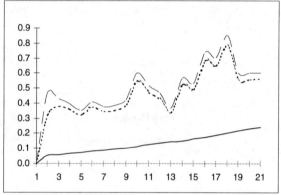

FIGURE 5.6. Mean response of volume to A shocks

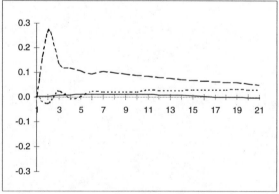

FIGURE 5.7. Volatility response of volume to A shocks

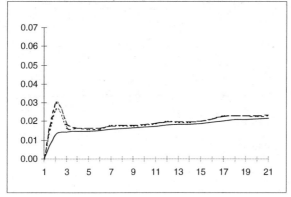

FIGURE 5.8. Mean response of price changes to B shocks

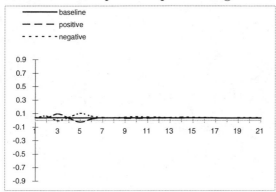

FIGURE 5.9. Volatility response of price changes to B shocks

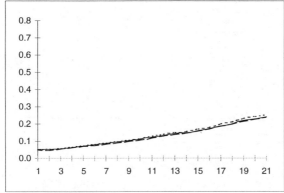

FIGURE 5.10. Mean response of volume to B shocks

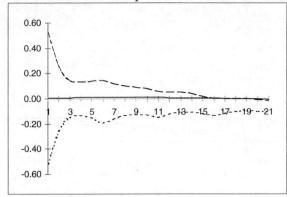

FIGURE 5.11. Volatility response of volume to B shocks

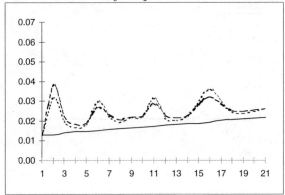

FIGURE 5.12. Mean response of price changes to C shocks

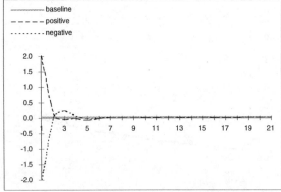

FIGURE 5.13. Volatility response of price changes to C shocks

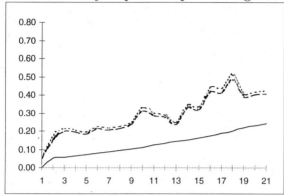

FIGURE 5.14. Mean response of volume to C shocks

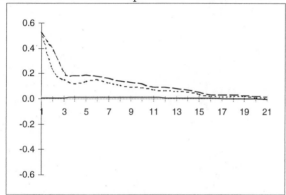

FIGURE 5.15. Volatility response of volume to C shocks

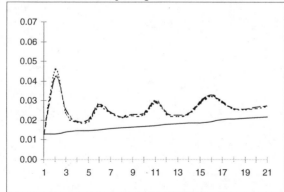

6
Testing the Structural Model

In this chapter we investigate to what extent the structural model developed in Section 3.3 can account for the observed joint dynamics of return and trading volume. We use the Efficient Method of Moment (EMM) estimator proposed by Bansal, Gallant, Hussey and Tauchen [5] and Gallant and Tauchen [34] to address this question. The EMM estimator provides a systematic way of developing moment conditions for estimation by simulation: It uses the score function of an auxiliary model, called the score generator, to define a criterion function for the Generalized Method of Moments (GMM) estimation (Hansen [39]).

The motivation of this exercise is twofold: First, existing economic models which generate volume in a framework of heterogeneous agents do not confront the data in their full complexity and have not evolved sufficiently to guide the specification of an empirical model of daily stock market data. Second, existing empirical work is to a large extent data-based. It is not guided by rigorous, dynamic equilibrium models of market behavior. It is more statistical than economic and typically neither the optimization problem agents face nor the information structure is

fully specified. In addition, most of the empirical work studying the relationship between stock returns and volume usually
focuses only on one qualitative feature seen in the data (e.g.,
Campbell, Grossman and Wang [10] study persistence of return
and volume, Brock and LeBaron [9] study price volatility and
volume).

The remainder of this chapter is organized as follows: Section
1 briefly reviews the structural model of stock return and volume which we want the data to confront. Section 2 describes the
Efficient Method of Moments (EMM) estimator. This approach
allows us to estimate and test the structural model in a systematic way: i.e., instead of selecting only one qualitative feature
seen in the data on an *ad hoc* basis as in most other work, we
investigate the extent to which this highly stylized asset pricing
model with a nontradable asset can account for the observed
joint dynamics of stock price and trading volume. In Section 3
we apply this method to estimate and test the structural model
described in Chapter 3. For the sake of completeness, we compare the results by fitting a stochastic volatility model for the
price changes to the same data set. Section 5 summarizes the
findings.

6.1   The Structural Model

The economic world described in 3.3 can be summarized as follows: All agents have the same preference, have rational expectations, are equally informed and they maximize their life time
utilities. There are two kinds of assets available to all traders
in the economy: the bond (riskless), which has a gross rate of
return of $R = 1 + r$ per share, and the stock (risky), which pays
dividend D_t per share in time t. There is a third kind of asset
which is risky and is available only for one type of traders. The
expected excess return of this asset equals Z_t. Denote the group
of traders who have the opportunity to invest in the risky asset not available to all traders as type A traders and the other
group of traders as type B traders. Suppose that D_t follows an

AR(1) process with a time-invariant conditional variance

$$D_t = a_D D_{t-1} + \epsilon_{D,t}, \quad \epsilon_{D,t} \sim i.i.d. \ N\left(0, \sigma_D^2\right) \qquad (6.1)$$

whereas Z_t follows an Autoregressive Conditional Heteroskedasticity (ARCH) process

$$Z_t = a_Z Z_{t-1} + \epsilon_{Z,t}, \quad \epsilon_{Z,t} \sim N(0, \sigma_{Z,t}^2), \qquad (6.2)$$

with $0 \le a_Z < 1$ and $\sigma_{Z,t}^2 = f\left(\sigma_{Z,t-1}^2; t\right)$. The equilibrium stock price is given by[1]

$$P_t = p_{0,t} + a D_t - p_{Z,t} Z_t, \qquad (6.3)$$

where $a = \frac{a_D}{R - a_D}$ and where $p_{0,t}$ and $p_{Z,t}$ are deterministic sequences. Furthermore, since within each type all agents are identical, stock trading volume is equal to the changes of the optimal stock demand aggregated through all agents of one of the two types. From Appendix B, the optimal stock demand of type B traders, denoted as X_t^B, is linear in Z_t:

$$X_t^B = f_{0,t}^B + f_{Z,t}^B Z_t, \qquad (6.4)$$

where $f_{0,t}^B$ and $f_{Z,t}^B$ are functions of $\sigma_{Z,t}^2$. Trading volume in time t can be written as $1 - \omega$ times the absolute changes of the optimal holding of stock from B type traders. Therefore, volume equals

$$
\begin{aligned}
V_t &= (1 - \omega)\left|X_t^B - X_{t-1}^B\right| \qquad (6.5)\\
&= (1 - \omega)\left|f_{0,t}^B - f_{0,t-1}^B + f_{Z,t}^B Z_t - f_{Z,t-1}^B Z_{t-1}\right|.
\end{aligned}
$$

6.2   Efficient Method of Moments

Gallant and Tauchen [34] develop a systematic approach to generating moment conditions for the generalized method of moments (GMM) estimator (Hansen [39]) of the parameters of a structural model. The method is an alternative to the common

---

[1] This equation is identical to equation (3.15).

practice of selecting a few low order moments on an *ad hoc* basis and then proceeding with the GMM. The basic idea of the EMM approach is that one uses the expectations under the structural model of the score from an auxiliary model (score generator) as the vector of moment conditions. If the score generator approximates the actual distribution of the data well, the estimator is nearly fully efficient even if the score generator does not encompass the structural model.

To illustrate, suppose there is a parametrized model for $y_t = (Q_t, V_t)'$. Let $\rho \in \Re \subset \Re^{p_\rho}$ denote an unknown $(p\rho \times 1)$ vector of parameters. Suppose the DGP for y_t is generated by the parametric model with the parameter ρ_0. Let $g(y_t, \rho)$ be a q-dimensional vector of functions, $g : (\Re^2 \times \Re^{p_\rho}) \to \Re^q$, which is designed in such a way that it has expectation zero for $\rho = \rho_0$, i.e.,

$$E\left[g(y_t, \rho_0)\right] = 0. \tag{6.6}$$

Suppose that a law of large numbers can be applied to $g(y_t, \rho)$ for admissible ρ, so that the sample mean of $g(y_t, \rho)$ converges to its population mean with probability one:

$$\lim_{n\to\infty} \frac{1}{n} \sum_{t=1}^{n} g(y_t, \rho) = E\left[g(y_t, \rho)\right] \tag{6.7}$$

where n is the sample size. The idea behind the GMM is to mimic the moment restrictions (6.6) with a sample mean by minimizing a quadratic form

$$Q_n(\rho) = \left[\frac{1}{n} \sum_{t=1}^{n} g(y_t, \rho)\right]' W_n \left[\frac{1}{n} \sum_{t=1}^{n} g(y_t, \rho)\right] \tag{6.8}$$

with respect to ρ, where W_n is a positive definite weighting matrix which satisfies

$$\lim_{n\to\infty} W_n = W_0 \tag{6.9}$$

with probability one for a positive definite matrix W_0. Then the GMM estimator, $\widehat{\rho}_n$, is the solution of the minimization problem (6.8). Under fairly general regularity conditions, the GMM estimator $\widehat{\rho}_n$ is a consistent estimator for ρ_0, with W_0 denoting arbitrary weighting matrices.

6.2.1 EMM Estimator

The idea behind the EMM estimator is the following: The parameters of the structural model is ρ, which is a vector of length $p\rho$. The observed data $\{y_t\}_{t=1}^{n}$ is presumed to have been generated by the structural model described by equations (6.1)-(6.5) for some value $\rho_0 \in R \subset \Re^{p\rho}$. The task is to estimate ρ_0 and test the specifications of the structural model.

Suppose a conditional density for y_t: $f(y_t|y_{t-L}, ..., y_{t-1}, \theta)$, with $\theta \in \Theta \subset \Re^{p\theta}$ and θ is a vector of length $p\theta$, is found to provide a good statistical description of the data. The conditional density $f(y_t|y_{t-L}, ..., y_{t-1}, \theta)$ is called the f-model. The f-model providing a good fit means that it is selected on the basis of a model selection criterion such as the Schwarz criterion and that is does well in a battery of statistical specification tests. In other words, the f-model provides a good approximation to the data generating process. In our application, we choose to use the bivariate SNP score described in Chapter 5 as the f-model.

The score function of the f-model is

$$s_f(y_{t-L}, ..., y_{t-1}, y_t, \theta) = \frac{\partial}{\partial \theta} \log\left[f(y_t|y_{t-L}, ..., y_{t-1}, \theta)\right]. \quad (6.10)$$

Given the realization $\{y_t\}_{t=1}^{n}$, the f-model is estimated by the quasi-maximum likelihood

$$\tilde{\theta}_n = \arg\max_{\theta \in \Theta} \frac{1}{n} \sum_{t=L+1}^{n} \log f(y_t|y_{t-L}, ..., y_{t-1}, \theta). \quad (6.11)$$

The first order condition is

$$\frac{\partial}{\partial \theta} \frac{1}{n} \sum_{t=L+1}^{n} \log f(y_t|y_{t-L}, ..., y_{t-1}, \theta) = 0, \quad (6.12)$$

or, equivalently,

$$\frac{1}{n} \sum_{t=L+1}^{n} s_f(y_{t-L}, ..., y_{t-1}, y_t, \tilde{\theta}_n) = 0. \quad (6.13)$$

The strategy of the EMM is to mimic the first order condition (6.13) induced by the quasi-maximum likelihood estimation (6.11) of the f-model: Since the left side of equation (6.13) is averaged over the observed realization $\{y_t\}_{t=1}^n$, a good estimator for ρ would be one that makes

$$\frac{1}{N} \sum_{\tau=L+1}^{N} s_f\left(\widehat{y}_{\tau-L}(\rho), ..., \widehat{y}_{\tau-1}(\rho), \widehat{y}_\tau(\rho), \widetilde{\theta}_n\right) \approx 0, \qquad (6.14)$$

with the average taken over the simulated realization $\{\widehat{y}_\tau(\rho)\}_{\tau=1}^{N}$ under the structural model. If $p\theta = p\rho$, equation (6.14) typically holds with equality. Typically it is the case that $p\theta > p\rho$, which means that (6.14) cannot in general hold with equality; this is the motivation behind GMM described before. Put

$$\widehat{m}_N\left(\rho, \widetilde{\theta}_n\right) = \frac{1}{N} \sum_{\tau=L+1}^{N} s_f\left(\widehat{y}_{\tau-L}(\rho), ..., \widehat{y}_{\tau-1}(\rho), \widehat{y}_\tau(\rho), \widetilde{\theta}_n\right),$$
$$(6.15)$$

which is the mean score of the f-model averaged with respect to the simulation $\{\widehat{y}_\tau(\rho)\}_{\tau=1}^{N}$. This is why the f-model is called the score generator. The EMM estimator is then given by

$$\widehat{\rho} = \arg\min_{\rho \in \Re} \left\{ \widehat{m}_N\left(\rho, \widetilde{\theta}_n\right)' \widetilde{W}_n^{-1} \widehat{m}_N\left(\rho, \widetilde{\theta}_n\right) \right\}, \qquad (6.16)$$

where $\widetilde{W}_n$ is a positive definite weighing matrix such that $\widetilde{W}_n \overset{as}{\rightarrow} W$ as $n \to \infty$. The estimator in (6.16) minimizes with respect to ρ the length of $\widehat{m}_N\left(\rho, \widetilde{\theta}_n\right)$ relative to $\left(\widetilde{W}_n\right)^{-1}$.

Under reasonable regularity conditions[2], $\widehat{\rho}$ is consistent and $\sqrt{n}\left(\widehat{\rho} - \rho_0\right)$ is asymptotically normal. The score generator need not encompass (nest) the structural model. If it does, then the estimator described above is as efficient as the maximum likelihood estimator. Hence, this approach ensures efficiency against

---

[2] See Gallant and Tauchen [34].

a given parametric model. If the score generator closely approximates the actual distribution of the data, even though it does not encompass it, the estimator is nearly fully efficient. Thus, the better the score generator approximates the conditional distribution of the data, the closer is the asymptotic covariance matrix to that of maximum likelihood.

The elements of $m_N\left(\widehat{\rho}, \widetilde{\theta}_n\right)$ contain diagnostic information on how well the structural model accounts for the scores of the f-model. Larger elements indicate those scores that it has trouble accounting for. Denote the diagonal elements of $\widetilde{W}_n$ as $\text{diag}\left(\widetilde{W}_n\right)$, one can use the quasi-$t$-ratios, the components of

$$\widehat{T}_n = \left[\left(\text{diag}\left(\widetilde{W}_n\right)\right)^{\frac{1}{2}}\right]^{-1} \sqrt{n} \cdot m_N\left(\widehat{\rho}, \widetilde{\theta}_n\right), \qquad (6.17)$$

which provide suggestive diagnostics to detect the characteristics of the data not matched by the structural model. A large quasi-t-ratio indicates that the structural model does a poor job of fitting that particular score.

6.3   Application of EMM

In this section we apply the EMM estimator to estimate and test the structural model described in Sections 3.3 and 6.1. The data used here are the daily Dow Jones Industrial Average and the number of shares traded on the New York Stock Exchange from 1/1/1952 to 9/30/1987 as described in Section 5.1.

6.3.1   Score Generator

As stated before, to implement the EMM estimator a score generator is required that approximates these data well. The investigation of Tauchen [72] indicates that a score generator based on nonparametric considerations would be more appropriate. He argues that only by using a flexible, nonparametric auxiliary model can one ensure that parameter estimates are fully efficient when the underlying structural model is true and that misspecification will be detected when the structural model is false. In our application we would like to have a score generator which, on the one hand, fully describes the data and, on the other hand, goes beyond the parametric models which are found to fit the data quite well (for example, ARCH/GARCH models), in order to avoid this problem. This is our reason for choosing the bivariate SNP score which is described in Chapter 5. As noted there, the SNP family is sufficiently rich to approximate closely any reasonably smooth conditional density.

As noted in Chapter 5, the SNP specification with $K_z > 0$, $K_x = 0$, $L_u > 0$ and $L_r > 0$ is a linear autoregression with an ARCH error structure and a homogeneous, nonparametric error density. It is very similar to the semiparametric GARCH model of Engle and Gonzales-Rivera [19], but with a more flexible specification for the ARCH component and the Hermite expansion used for the error density. Relaxing the restriction $K_x = 0$ permits conditional heterogeneity to enter the error density. In our application, we choose two SNP specifications as the score generators: the primary model found in Section 5.2.2, i.e., the model with $L_u = 5$, $L_r = 17$, $L_p = 1$, $K_z = 9$, $I_z = 2$, $K_x = 2$, $I_x = 1$ (denoted as "Nonlinear/Nonparametric score" below) and the Hannan-Quinn preferred model, i.e., the model with $L_u = 6$, $L_r = 17$, $L_p = 0$, $K_z = 9$, $I_z = 2$, $K_x = 0$, $I_x = 0$ (denoted as "Nonparametric ARCH score" below). These two SNP specifications generate two score generators for the structural model to confront.

6.3.2 Estimation of the Structural Model

The structural model we want to estimate is described in equation (3.11) and (3.18). In our empirical effort we make the following approximation to make the estimation of the structural model easier: we approximate the coefficient $p_{Z,t}$ by an affine function of σ_t^{-1}

$$p_{Z,t} \approx p_0 + \frac{p_1}{\sigma_t} \tag{6.18}$$

where $p_0 > 0$ and $p_1 > 0$ are constants. This approximation is justified by the following two benchmark cases: First, in the case of unconditional Gaussian shocks, the coefficient p_Z in equation (3.15) is inversely related to σ_Z.[3] Second, if the preference of the agents is myopic, i.e., instead of (3.5), agents face the following maximization problem

$$\max E_t \left[- \exp \gamma \left(W_{t+1} \right) \right]$$
$$\text{s. t. } W_{t+1} = W_t R + \mathbf{X}'_t \mathbf{Q}_{t+1}$$

where $E_t \left(\cdot \right)$ denotes the expectation conditional on time t information set, γ is the absolute risk aversion coefficient, W_t denotes the wealth, $\mathbf{X}_t$ denotes the optimal holdings of the risky assets and $\mathbf{Q}_{t+1}$ is the expected returns on the risky assets. One can get an explicit solution for $p_{Z,t}$ which has the form as in (6.18) when the distributional assumption is identical to that in the structural model described in Section 3.3 and 6.1, i.e., the expected return on the nontradable asset (Z_t) has a time-varying volatility.

Given equation (6.18) for $p_{Z,t}$, the expected value of $\widetilde{Q}_{t+1} \equiv Q_{t+1} - p_{0,t+1} + R p_{0,t}$, i.e. the random part of excess return, can be written as

$$E_t \left(\widetilde{Q}_{t+1} \right) = \left(R p_{Z,t} - a_Z p_{Z,t+1} \right) Z_t$$
$$= \left(R - a_Z \right) p_0 + \left(\frac{R}{\sigma_t} - \frac{a_Z}{\sigma_{t+1}} \right) Z_t \quad (6.19)$$

by using equation (3.16).

---

[3] This can be shown by rewriting the variance of the dividend (σ_D^2) as well as that of the return on the nontradable asset (σ_q^2) as proportional to σ_Z^2, i.e., $\sigma_D^2 \equiv \delta^2 \sigma_Z^2$ and $\sigma_q^2 \equiv \varpi^2 \sigma_Z^2$. Because of equations (A.6) and (A.7) in Appendix A, the solution for v_2^A and v_2^B has the form

$$v_2^A = \frac{\lambda^A}{\sigma_Z^2} \text{ and } v_2^B = \frac{\lambda^B}{\sigma_Z^2}$$

where λ^A and λ^B are some constants independent of σ_Z^2. Now substitute the solution for v_2^A as well as v_2^B into equation (A.8), we get a polynomial in p_Z which has the form

$$\Pi \left(p_Z \right) \equiv \left(p_Z \right)^3 - \frac{\pi_2}{\sigma_Z} \left(p_Z \right)^2 + \pi_1 p_Z - \frac{\pi_0}{\sigma_Z} = 0$$

where π_0, π_1 and π_2 are some constants independent of σ_Z^2. From the above equation, $\Pi \left(p_Z = p_Z^*, \sigma_Z = \hat{\sigma}_Z \right) > \Pi \left(p_Z = p_Z^*, \sigma_Z = \tilde{\sigma}_Z \right)$ for all $p_Z^* \geq 0$ and $\hat{\sigma}_Z > \tilde{\sigma}_Z > 0$. Therefore, the positive solution for p_Z in the equation above is negatively related to σ_Z.

The autoregressive parameters for stock dividend (a_D) as well as for the nontradable asset (a_Z) are set equal to one. This makes the returns on risky assets a random walk. In daily data any plausible dividend process will have a_D close to one.[4] In addition, stock returns are known to have small autocorrelation[5] and the estimation is simplified by setting a_D and a_Z equal to one. The rate of return for the riskless asset r is set to be zero. For the variance the following specification is adopted

$$\sigma_t = w_0 + w_1 \sigma_{t-1}$$

where w_0 and w_1 are constants. Volume data have been found to be very persistent (among others, Campbell et al [10] and Gallant et al [32]), we assume that volume series can be well approximated by the lagged volume and the absolute value of return. Therefore, the final model the data confront consists of four equations:

$$
\begin{aligned}
Z_t &= Z_{t-1} + \sigma_t \varepsilon_{Z,t}, \\
\sigma_t &= w_0 + w_1 \sigma_{t-1}, \\
Q_{t+1} &= p_0 + p_1 \left(\frac{1}{\sigma_t} - \frac{1}{\sigma_{t+1}} \right) Z_t + u_t, \\
V_t &= \beta_0 + \beta_1 V_{t-1} + \beta_2 |Q_t| + \eta_t,
\end{aligned}
$$

where $u_t \sim i.i.d.N\left(0, \sigma_u^2\right)$ is the innovation in the excess return, which is a linear function of $\varepsilon_{D,t}$ and $\varepsilon_{Z,t}$, and $\eta_t \sim i.i.d.N\left(0, \sigma_\eta^2\right)$ represents other disturbances in the return and volume data which are assumed to be independent with u_t and $\varepsilon_{Z,t}$. The parameter vector to be estimated is

$$\rho = (p_0, p_1, \beta_0, \beta_1, \beta_2, w_0, w_1, \sigma_u, \sigma_\eta)'.$$

The program code for EMM estimation is kindly provided by Gallant and Tauchen which is available via ftp.[6] We choose to

---

[4] This value is also taken in the simulation exercise by Campbell, Grossman and Wang [10] in which daily data are used.

[5] This can be seen from the nonlinear impulse response analysis conducted in Chapter 4: the mean responses of stock price to its own shocks are heavily dampend and return to the baseline after one day. See Figure 5.4.

[6] A fortran program implementing the EMM method is available via anonymous ftp at ftp.econ.duke.edu (152.3.10.64).

simulate $15,000 \ (= N)$ realizations and discard the first $1,000$ values in order to let the effects of transients associated with the initial conditions for ρ_0 die out. The weighting matrix chosen here is the one suggested by Gallant and Tauchen [34] based on the mean outer product of the gradient

$$\widetilde{W}_n = \frac{1}{n} \sum_{t=L+1}^{n} s_f \left(\widetilde{y}_{t-L}, ..., \widetilde{y}_{t-1}, \widetilde{y}_t, \widetilde{\theta} \right) s_f \left(\widetilde{y}_{t-L}, ..., \widetilde{y}_{t-1}, \widetilde{y}_t, \widetilde{\theta} \right)'.$$

We now turn to our empirical results. First, the volatility is highly persistent with $\widehat{w}_1 = 0.919$. Persistent conditional variance is a common finding in the empirical literature using high frequency stock returns. The estimates of p_0 and p_1 are positive ($\widehat{p}_0 = 0.162$, $\widehat{p}_1 = 0.177$), which confirms the implication of the structural model. Furthermore, volume is positively related to the absolute value of price ($\widehat{\beta}_2 = 0.216$). Therefore, our result confirms the previous empirical studies in which a persistent return volatility and a positive relation between volume and the absolute value of price changes are found. However, the large χ^2 statistics ($\chi^2(89) = 645$) indicates that the simple asset pricing model as a whole fails to approximate the bivariate distribution of price changes and volume completely. When dropping the homogeneity constraint, i.e., using the Nonlinear-Nonparametric score, the structural model is overwhelmingly rejected ($\chi^2(248) = 48,006$).

As noted before, the EMM quasi-t-ratios

$$\widehat{T}_n = \left[\left(\text{diag} \left(\widetilde{W}_n \right) \right)^{\frac{1}{2}} \right]^{-1} \sqrt{n} \cdot m_N \left(\widehat{\rho}, \widetilde{\theta}_n \right)$$

provide suggestive diagnostics. In order to get an insight of the characteristics of the data that the structural model cannot approximate, we display the EMM quasi-t-ratios as barcharts in Figure 6.1 to 6.6 under the Nonlinear/Nonparametric score. A quasi-t-statistic above 2.0 indicates failure to fit the corresponding score, which is particularly useful for assessing the underlying causes of a statistically significant chi-square statistic. As we can see from the figures, the model seems to match the moments

of the AR parameters. The ARCH part of the nonparametric
scores is also matched quite well except for the second term of
the price series. The main failure lies in the Hermite polynomial
part of the SNP score, which indicates that the simulated data
generated by the structural model are conditionally too close to
the Gaussian distribution relative to the observed data.

One possible reason for the unsuccessful matching between
the structural model and the score generator is that return and
volume series have very different characteristics: the return data
have very heavy tails and the autocorrelation coefficients of the
return series are very small. The volume data, however, do not
have heavy tails but are very persistent. Moreover, the autocorrelations from the squared residuals of the return series are
large and eight out of the first ten autocorrelations coefficients
are significant. This can be seen from Table 5.1 or from the results of our nonlinear impulse response analysis in Chapter 5.
To adopt the persistence in the volatility of return series and the
persistence of volume series, we modify the structural model to
the following

$$Z_t = Z_{t-1} + \sigma_t \varepsilon_{Z,t},$$
$$\sigma_t = w_0 + w_1 \sigma_{t-1},$$
$$Q_{t+1} = p_0 + p_1 \left[\left(\frac{1}{\sigma_t} - \frac{1}{\sigma_{t-1}} \right) Z_{t-1} \right] + u_t,$$
$$V_t = \beta_0 + \beta_1 V_{t-1} + \beta_2 V_{t-2} + \beta_3 |\Delta Q_t| + \eta_t,$$

so that more lags are incorporated in the variance equation of
price changes and in the volume series. However, the result can
hardly be called a success ($\chi^2(86) = 728$).

6.4   Does The Stochastic Volatility Model Do Better?

The stochastic volatility model has been proposed to describe
the dynamics short-term financial data (Clark [14], Tauchen
and Pitts [73], Taylor [75]). It takes the form of an autoregres-

sive model whose innovations are scaled by an unobservable autoregression. If the state variables in the structural model, e.g. return on the nontradable asset, follows a stochastic volatility model, there is no explicit solution for the dynamic optimization problem described in Chapter 3. In other words, we regard the stochastic volatility model as a statistical rather than as an economic model. It is however an interesting exercise to see if the stochastic volatility model would fit the data better than the ARCH-GARCH model because of the increasing number of applications of the stochastic volatility model in the empirical finance.

Therefore, Q_t is now assumed to follow the process

$$Q_t - \mu = \phi (Q_{t-1} - \mu) + \exp (w_t) \sigma z_{1t} \qquad (6.20)$$

$$w_t - \mu_w = c (w_{t-1} - \mu_w) + \sigma_w z_{2t} \qquad (6.21)$$

where z_{it} are independent i.i.d. Gaussian processes with $z_{it} \sim N(0,1)$, $i = 1, 2$. The equation for volume is

$$V_t = \beta_0 + \beta_1 V_{t-1} + \beta_2 V_{t-2} + \beta_3 |Q_t| + \eta_t \qquad (6.22)$$

with $\eta_t \sim i.i.d. N (0, \sigma \eta^2)$ independent of z_{it}, $i = 1, 2$. One implication of the stochastic volatility model[7] is that the kurtosis of the unconditional distribution

$$\begin{aligned} \kappa &\equiv \frac{E(Q_t - \mu_{t-1,t})^4}{[\text{Var}(Q_t - \mu_{t-1,t})]^2} \\ &= 3 \exp [4\text{Var}(w_t)], \end{aligned}$$

with

$$\mu_{t-1,t} \equiv \phi (Q_{t-1} - \mu) + \mu$$

is larger than 3 if w_t is not a degenerated random variable. The model can also accommodate excess kurtosis in the conditional distribution of Q_t: Gallant et al. [29] show that

$$\kappa_t \equiv \frac{\left[E \left(Q_t - \mu_{t-1,t} \mid \{Q_{t-j}\}_{j=-\infty}^{t-1} \right) \right]^4}{\left[\text{Var} \left(Q_t - \mu_{t-1,t} \mid \{Q_{t-j}\}_{j=-\infty}^{t-1} \right) \right]^2} > 3.$$

---

[7] See for example Gallant, Hsieh and Tauchen [29].

Thus, the model can account for the thick-tailed character of the unconditional distribution of Q_t. In addition, it can accommodate conditional heterogeneity, i.e.,

$$\frac{\left[Q_t - E\left(Q_t \mid \{Q_j\}_{j=-\infty}^{t-1}\right)\right]}{\sqrt{\text{Var}\left(Q_t \mid \{Q_j\}_{j=-\infty}^{t-1}\right)}}$$

is in general not an $i.i.d.$ process.

Using the EMM method described before, we fit the stochastic volatility model (6.20), (6.21) and (6.22) to the same data set. Again, we use the two SNP specifications as auxiliary models. Unfortunately, the stochastic volatility model fails to approximate the distribution of these data: For the nonparametric ARCH specification the chi-square statistic is $\chi^2(87) = 15,080$ and for the Nonlinear/Nonparametric specification it is $\chi^2(246) = 50,588$; it is overwhelmingly rejected.[8]

6.5   Summary

In this chapter we have applied the EMM estimator to estimate and test the structural model described in Section 3.3 and 6.1. The asset pricing model with a time-varying volatility for the return on the nontradable asset failed to fit the data completely. We have found that the model can match most of the moments of the variance function and the moments of the mean function of the SNP Nonparametric ARCH score, but not the moments of the Hermite polynomial part. However, the estimation results of the highly stylized structural model are in line with findings of previous empirical work.

---

[8] The quasi-t-ratios of the stochastic volatility model show that this model can match neither the moments of the AR parameters nor those of the ARCH part for the return series. For the volume series the problem is even more serious.

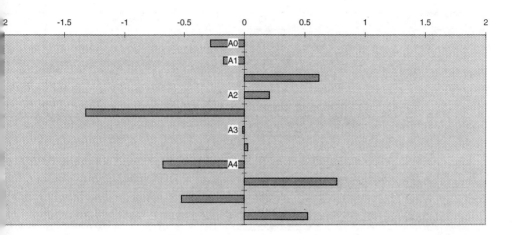

FIGURE 6.1. VAR t-ratios of returns

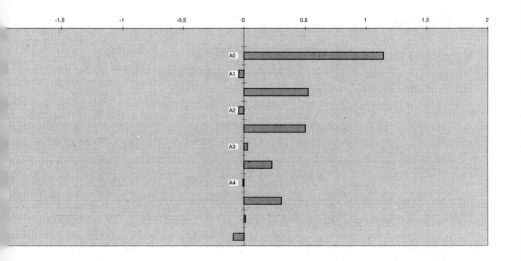

FIGURE 6.2. VAR t-ratios of volume

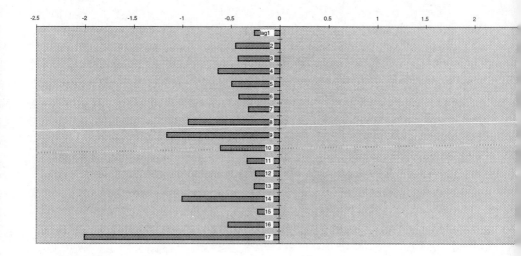

FIGURE 6.3. ARCH t-ratios of returns

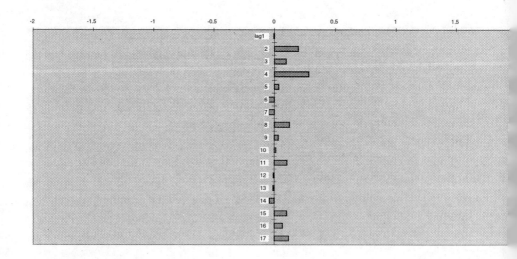

FIGURE 6.4. ARCH t-ratios of volume

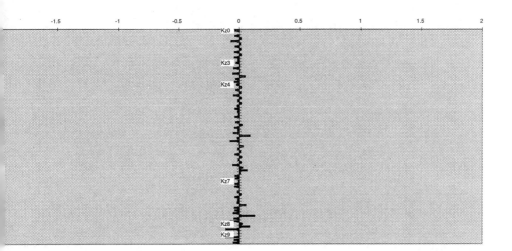

FIGURE 6.5. SNP t-ratios of returns

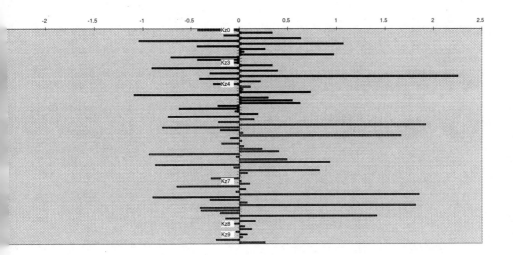

FIGURE 6.6. SNP t-ratios of volume

7
Conclusions

The theme of this manuscript has been to investigate the joint dynamics of stock returns and trading volume. The main contribution is twofold. First, we propose a fully dynamic model in which agents have rational expectations and are equally informed. Trade occurs in this economy because of the different investment opportunities among the agents. We showed that if the return on the nontradable asset has a deterministic but time-varying volatility, there is a steady state rational expectations equilibrium in which the market clearing price is linear in the payoffs of the risky assets. The immediate gain from assuming a time-varying volatility is that the stock returns would have a distribution much closer to what we observe in the data. Ideally, we would use a time-varying stochastic volatility. However, if the volatility is stochastic, there is no closed form solution for the intertemporal optimization problem because the form of the value function is unknown. Therefore, the analysis of the dynamics between volume and return becomes intractable. With a deterministic time-varying volatility, we show that there is a rational expectations equilibrium in which the market clearing price is linear in the returns of the risky assets in the economy.

We present numerical evidence that this economy can mimic the stochastic volatility properties of financial returns. This suggests that the assumption of deterministic volatility might be a reasonable first approximation. We show analytically that the predicted relation between the serial correlation of stock returns and volume is not monotonic: it can be positive or negative, depending on the probability structure of the shocks. This result can explain the controversial findings in empirical literature studying the relation between volume and the persistence of stock returns. The relation between volume and volatility is more complicated and cannot be derived analytically. Thus, we rely on the numerical exercises. In the simulations to be reported below, we model the deterministic volatility process by the chaotic tent map dynamics which is known to behave similar as an AR(1) process (Sakai and Tokumaru, [63]). The simulated stock return mimics the GARCH behavior quite well. Thus, as noted above, modelling the volatility as an autocorrelated time-varying deterministic process can be viewed as an approximation to the ARCH or GARCH process (Engle, [18], Bollerslev, [7]) which is one of the most prominent tools for characterizing changing variance of financial time series. The ambiguous relation between the serial correlation of stock return and volume as well as the positive relation between volume and the volatility of stock return are confirmed in a series of empirical and numerical examples. Therefore, the data generated from the simple dynamic asset pricing model with a time-varying volatility can mimic the volume-persistence and volume-volatility relation revealed in the observed data well.

Second, instead of focusing on one or a few qualitative features seen in the data, we investigated the extent to which this simple asset pricing model can account for the observed joint dynamics of stock returns and volume. This model is confronted with daily data on the Dow Jones Industrial Average and total NYSE trading volume from 1/1/1952 to 9/30/1987.

Nonparametric methods were used in most part of the empirical exercise. The SNP estimation technique was employed to fit the bivariate conditional density of stock returns and volume.

The result shows a complicated structure of the bivariate conditional density which is non Gaussian and nonlinear. The EMM method was applied to investigate systematically the extent to which the economic model introduced in Sections 3.3 and 6.1 can describe the characteristics of the data. Two stylized facts found by many previous empirical studies in high-frequency stock data were reproduced in the framework of this simple asset pricing model: (i) positive relation between volume and return (ii) persistent stock return volatility. Unfortunately, the model failed to fit the data completely: it can match most of the moments of the mean and the variance part of the nonparametric ARCH score, but not the moments of the Hermite polynomial part.

It is too much to expect this highly stylized asset pricing model with ARCH-GARCH innovations to be capable of fully explaining the complicated nonlinear structure of the observed data. However, a nice feature of the structural model proposed in Chapter 3 is that it allows a large class of time-varying volatility processes if the volatility is deterministic. Using the Efficient Method of Moment, Gallant, Hsieh and Tauchen [30] shows that the result by fitting the variance with a chaotic Mackey-Glass sequence is better than a standard stochastic volatility model for daily Standard and Poor's Composite Price Index. Whether this modification can fit the data better without losing the spirit of the structural model is an issue which we are still working on.

To conclude, it remains an interesting challenge to develop an equilibrium model with dynamic optimizing, heterogeneous and rational agents which can jointly account for major stylized facts: serially correlated stock returns, conditional heterogeneity of stock returns, contemporaneous volume-volatility and volume-persistence correlations.

Appendix A
Proof of Proposition 1

Define

$$
\begin{aligned}
\epsilon_{D,t} &= \delta\varepsilon_{D,t} \\
\epsilon_{Z,t} &= \sigma_t\varepsilon_{z,t} \\
\epsilon_{q,t} &= \kappa\varepsilon_{q,t}
\end{aligned}
$$

where $\sigma_t^2 = f\left(\sigma_{t-1}^2; t\right)$. If the price takes the conjectured form as in equation (3.15)

$$
P_t = p_{0,t} + aD_t - p_{Z,t}Z_t,
$$

the excess return per share of the stock Q_{t+1} equals

$$
\begin{aligned}
Q_{t+1} &= p_{0,t+1} - Rp_{0,t} + [Rp_{Z,t} - a_Zp_{Z,t+1}]\, Z_t \qquad \text{(A.1)} \\
&\quad + (1+a)\,\epsilon_{D,t+1} - p_{Z,t+1}\epsilon_{Z,t+1}.
\end{aligned}
$$

Define $\Psi_t \equiv (1, Z_t)'$, Ψ_t can be written as

$$
\Psi_t = a_\Psi\Psi_{t-1} + b_{\Psi,t}\epsilon_t,
$$

with $a_{\Psi} = \begin{pmatrix} 1 & 0 \\ 0 & a_Z \end{pmatrix}$, $b_{\Psi,t} = \begin{pmatrix} 0 & 0 & 0 \\ 0 & 1 & 0 \end{pmatrix}$ and

$$\epsilon_t \equiv \begin{pmatrix} \epsilon_{D,t} & \epsilon_{Z,t} & \epsilon_{q,t} \end{pmatrix}' \sim N\left(0, \Sigma_t\right), \quad \Sigma_t = \begin{pmatrix} \delta^2 & 0 & \rho \\ 0 & \sigma_t^2 & 0 \\ \rho & 0 & \kappa^2 \end{pmatrix}.$$

The excess returns of the type A traders $\mathcal{Q}_{t+1}^A = (Q_{t+1}, q_{t+1})'$ can be written as

$$\mathcal{Q}_{t+1}^A = \mathbf{e}_{\mathcal{Q}}^A \Psi_t + \mathbf{b}_{\mathcal{Q}}^A \epsilon_{t+1}, \tag{A.2}$$

with

$$\mathbf{e}_{\mathcal{Q}}^A = \begin{pmatrix} 0 & Rp_{Z,t} - a_Z p_{Z,t+1} \\ 0 & 1 \end{pmatrix}; \quad \mathbf{b}_{\mathcal{Q}}^A = \begin{pmatrix} 1+a & -p_{Z,t+1} & 0 \\ 0 & 0 & 1 \end{pmatrix}.$$

Analogously, the excess returns of the type B traders $\mathcal{Q}_{t+1}^B = Q_{t+1}$ can be written as

$$\mathcal{Q}_{t+1}^B = \mathbf{e}_{\mathcal{Q}}^B \Psi_t + \mathbf{b}_{\mathcal{Q}}^B \epsilon_{t+1}, \tag{A.3}$$

with

$$\mathbf{e}_{\mathcal{Q}}^B = \begin{pmatrix} 0 & Rp_{Z,t} - a_Z p_{Z,t+1} \end{pmatrix}; \quad \mathbf{b}_{\mathcal{Q}}^B = \begin{pmatrix} 1+a & -p_{Z,t+1} & 0 \end{pmatrix}$$

With this notation, both the A type and B type traders' optimization problem can be expressed in the form of the Bellman equation

$$\begin{aligned} & J\left(W_t; \Psi_t; t\right) \\ = & \max\left\{-\beta^t e^{-\gamma c_t} + E\left[J\left(W_{t+1}; \Psi_{t+1}; t+1\right) \mid \mathfrak{I}_t\right]\right\} \end{aligned}$$

subject to $W_{t+1} = (W_t - c_t) R + \mathbf{X}_t' \mathcal{Q}_{t+1}$.

This equation must hold for all $0 < t \leq T$. Because of the salvage term in equation (3.5) we have

$$J\left(W_{T+1}, \Psi_{T+1}; T+1\right) = -\beta^{T+1} e^{-\alpha W_{T+1}}. \tag{A.4}$$

The trial solution for the value function considered here is

$$J\left(W_t; \Psi_t; t\right) = -\beta^t e^{-\frac{r\gamma}{R}W_t - \frac{1}{2}\Psi_t'\mathbf{v}_t\Psi_t} \tag{A.5}$$

where $\mathbf{v}_t$ is a 2 by 2 matrix of following form

$$\mathbf{v}_t^i = \left(\begin{array}{cc} v_{1,t}^i & v_{3,t}^i \\ v_{3,t}^i & v_{2,t}^i \end{array} \right),$$

for $i = A, B$, Define

$$\begin{aligned}
\mathbf{v}_{aa,t+1}^i &\equiv a_\Psi' \mathbf{v}_{t+1}^i a_\Psi \\
\mathbf{v}_{ab,t+1}^i &\equiv a_\Psi' \mathbf{v}_{t+1}^i b_\Psi \\
\mathbf{v}_{bb,t+1}^i &\equiv b_\Psi' \mathbf{v}_{t+1}^i b_\Psi,
\end{aligned}$$

for $i = A, B$. It follows from equation (A.4) $\mathbf{v}_{T+1}^A = \mathbf{v}_{T+1}^B = 0$. In the exactly the same way as in Wang (A 18), page 161, one can derive the recursive equation[1]

$$\begin{aligned}
v_{1,t}^A &= \frac{1}{R}\left[v_{1,t+1}^A - \left(v_{3,t+1}^A\right)^2 s_{t+1}^A + \frac{\kappa^2}{\Delta_{t+1}^A}\left(\pi_{t+1} - p_{Z,t+1}v_{3,t+1}s_{t+1}^A\right)^2 \right] \\
&\quad + 2\left(\frac{r}{R}\ln r - \frac{1}{R}\ln\beta\sqrt{\frac{s_{t+1}^A}{\sigma_{t+1}^2}} - \ln R \right) \\[2mm]
v_{2,t}^A &= \frac{a_Z^2 v_{2,t+1}^A}{R}\left(1 - v_{2,t+1}^A s_{t+1}^A\right) \\
&\quad + \frac{\kappa^2\left[Rp_{Z,t} - a_Z p_{Z,t+1}\left(1 - v_{2,t+1}^A s_{t+1}^A\right)\right]^2}{R\Delta_{t+1}^A} \\
&\quad - \frac{2\left(1 + a\right)\rho\left[Rp_{Z,t} - a_Z p_{Z,t+1}\left(1 - v_{2,t+1}^A s_{t+1}^A\right)\right]}{R\Delta_{t+1}^A} \\
&\quad + \frac{\left(1 + a\right)^2\delta^2 + p_{Z,t+1}^2 s_{t+1}^A}{R\Delta_{t+1}^A} \\[2mm]
v_{3,t}^A &= \frac{a_Z v_{3,t+1}^A}{R}\left(1 - v_{2,t+1}^A s_{t+1}^A\right) \\
&\quad + \frac{\kappa^2\left(\pi_{t+1} - p_{Z,t+1}v_{3,t+1}^A s_{t+1}^A\right)\left[Rp_{Z,t} - a_Z p_{Z,t+1}\left(1 - v_{2,t+1}^A s_{t+1}^A\right)\right]^2}{R\Delta_{t+1}^A}
\end{aligned} \tag{A.6}$$

---

[1] There seems to be a typo in Wang's equation (A17) and (A18) on page 161.

$$-\frac{(1+a)\,\rho\left(\pi_{t+1}-p_{Z,t+1}v_{3,t+1}^A s_{t+1}^A\right)}{R\Delta_{t+1}^A}$$

$$
\begin{aligned}
v_{1,t}^B &= \frac{1}{R}\left[v_{1,t+1}^B-\left(v_{3,t+1}^B\right)^2 s_{t+1}^B+\frac{1}{\Delta_{t+1}^B}\left(\pi_{t+1}-p_{Z,t+1}v_{3,t+1}^B s_{t+1}^B\right)^2\right]\\
&\quad+2\left(\frac{r}{R}\ln r-\frac{1}{R}\ln\beta\sqrt{\frac{s_{t+1}^A}{\sigma_{t+1}^2}}-\ln R\right)\\[4pt]
v_{2,t}^B &= \frac{a_Z^2 v_{2,t+1}^B}{R}\left(1-v_{2,t+1}^B s_{t+1}^B\right)\\
&\quad+\frac{\left[Rp_{Z,t}-a_Z p_{Z,t+1}\left(1-v_{2,t+1}^B s_{t+1}^B\right)\right]^2}{R\Delta_{t+1}^B}\\[4pt]
v_{3,t}^B &= \frac{a_Z v_{3,t+1}^B}{R}\left(1-v_{2,t+1}^B s_{t+1}^B\right)\\
&\quad+\frac{\left(\pi_{t+1}-p_{Z,t+1}v_{3,t+1}^B s_{t+1}^B\right)\left[Rp_{Z,t}-a_Z p_{Z,t+1}\left(1-v_{2,t+1}^B s_{t+1}^B\right)\right]}{R\Delta_{t+1}^B}
\end{aligned}
$$

(A

where

$$
\begin{aligned}
s_{t+1}^A &= \frac{\sigma_{t+1}^2}{1+v_{2,t+1}^A \sigma_{t+1}^2}\\[4pt]
s_{t+1}^B &= \frac{\sigma_{t+1}^2}{1+v_{2,t+1}^B \sigma_{t+1}^2}\\[4pt]
\Delta_{t+1}^A &= (1+a)^2\left(\delta^2\kappa^2-\rho^2\right)+\kappa^2 p_{Z,t+1}^2 s_{t+1}^A\\
\Delta_{t+1}^B &= (1+a)^2\delta^2+p_{Z,t+1}^2 s_{t+1}^B\\
\pi_{t+1} &= p_{0,t+1}-Rp_{0,t}
\end{aligned}
$$

Moreover, from the market clearing condition

$$\omega X_t^A+(1-\omega)X_t^B=1$$

one can derive the following two additional equations:

$$p_{0,t}=\frac{1}{R}\left[p_{0,t+1}-\frac{\omega\kappa^2\Delta_{t+1}^B s_{t+1}^A v_{3,t+1}^A+(1-\omega)\Delta_{t+1}^A s_{t+1}^B v_{3,t+1}^B+\alpha\Delta_{t+1}^A\Delta_{t-}^B}{\omega\kappa^2\Delta_{t+1}^B+(1-\omega)\Delta_{t+1}^A}\right.$$

$$t \quad = \quad \frac{a_Z p_{Z,t+1} \left[\omega \kappa^2 \Delta_{t+1}^B \left(1 - s_{t+1}^A v_{2,t+1}^A \right) + (1 - \omega) \Delta_{t+1}^A \left(1 - s_{t+1}^B v_{2,t+1}^B \right) \right]}{R \left[\omega \kappa^2 \Delta_{t+1}^B + (1 - \omega) \Delta_{t+1}^A \right]}$$

$$+ \frac{\omega \left(1 + a \right) \rho \Delta_{t+1}^B}{R \left[\omega \kappa^2 \Delta_{t+1}^B + (1 - \omega) \Delta_{t+1}^A \right]} \tag{A.8}$$

This system of first order difference equations can be solved backwards with the end condition $v_{T+1}^A = v_{T+1}^B = 0$. ∎

Appendix B
Proof of Proposition 2

Since trading volume in time t can be written as

$$V_t = (1 - \omega) \left| f_{0,t}^B - f_{0,t-1}^B + f_{Z,t}^B Z_t - f_{Z,t-1}^B Z_{t-1} \right|,$$

define $Y_t \equiv f_{0,t}^B - f_{0,t-1}^B + f_{Z,t}^B Z_t - f_{Z,t-1}^B Z_{t-1}$. Then Y_t is normal distributed as $Y_t \sim N \left(\mu_t, \left[f_{Z,t}^B \right]^2 \chi_t^2 + \left[f_{Z,t-1}^B \right]^2 \chi_{t-1}^2 \right)$ with $\mu_t \equiv f_{0,t}^B - f_{0,t-1}^B$ and $\chi_t^2 = \sum_{j=0}^{\infty} a_Z^j \sigma_{t-j}^2$. Denote the covariance matrix

of $\left(\widetilde{Q}_{t+1}, \left(\widetilde{Q}_t, Y_t \right)' \right)$ by $\Sigma_t \equiv \begin{pmatrix} \Sigma_{aa,t} & \Sigma_{ab,t} \\ \Sigma_{ba,t} & \Sigma_{bb,t} \end{pmatrix}$. Using a similar argument as in Appendix B of Wang (also see below), one can derive the following result which is the counter part of equation (B 10) in Wang (1994), page 165, with time-varying volatility:

$$E \left(\widetilde{Q}_{t+1} \mid \widetilde{Q}_t, V_t \right) \tag{B.1}$$

$$= \Sigma_{ab,t} \Sigma_{bb,t}^{-1} \left[\begin{pmatrix} \widetilde{Q}_t \\ -\mu_t \end{pmatrix} + \begin{pmatrix} 0 \\ V_t \end{pmatrix} G \left(\widetilde{Q}_t, V_t, \mu_t \right) \right]$$

where

$$G \left(\widetilde{Q}_t, V_t, \mu_t \right) = \frac{f_1 - f_2}{f_1 + f_2},$$

and

$$f_1 = \exp\left[-\frac{1}{2}\left(\begin{array}{c}\widetilde{Q}_t \\ V_t - \mu_t\end{array}\right)' \Sigma_{bb,t}^{-1}\left(\begin{array}{c}\widetilde{Q}_t \\ V_t - \mu_t\end{array}\right)\right];$$

$$f_2 = \exp\left[-\frac{1}{2}\left(\begin{array}{c}\widetilde{Q}_t \\ -V_t - \mu_t\end{array}\right)' \Sigma_{bb,t}^{-1}\left(\begin{array}{c}\widetilde{Q}_t \\ -V_t - \mu_t\end{array}\right)\right].$$

The Taylor expansion with respect to $\widetilde{Q}_t$ and V_t of the right hand side of (B.1) is

$$E\left(\widetilde{Q}_{t+1} \mid \widetilde{Q}_t, V_t\right) = \lambda_{0,t+1} + \lambda_{1,t+1}V_t^2 + \lambda_{2,t+1}\widetilde{Q}_t + \lambda_{3,t+1}V_t^2\widetilde{Q}_t$$
$$+ \text{ high-order terms}$$

where

$$\lambda_{0,t+1} = -\left(\kappa_{Q_{t+1},Q_t}h_{Q_t,Y_t} + \kappa_{Q_{t+1},Y_t}h_{Y_t,Y_t}\right)\mu_t;$$
$$\lambda_{1,t+1} = -\left(\kappa_{Q_{t+1},Q_t}h_{Q_t,Y_t} + \kappa_{Q_{t+1},Y_t}h_{Y_t,Y_t}\right)h_{Y_t,Y_t}\mu_t;$$
$$\lambda_{2,t+1} = \kappa_{Q_{t+1},Q_t}h_{Q_t,Q_t} + \kappa_{Q_{t+1},Y_t}h_{Q_t,Y_t};$$
$$\lambda_{3,t+1} = \left(\kappa_{Q_{t+1},Q_t}h_{Q_t,Y_t} + \kappa_{Q_{t+1},Y_t}h_{Y_t,Y_t}\right)h_{Q_t,Y_t};$$
$$\kappa_{Q_{t+1},Q_t} = (Rp_{Z,t-1} - a_Z p_{Z,t})(Rp_{Z,t} - a_Z p_{Z,t+1})a_Z\chi_{t-1}^2$$
$$+p_{Z,t}(a_Z p_{Z,t+1} - rp_{Z,t})\sigma_t^2;$$
$$\kappa_{Q_{t+1},Y_t} = a_z(Rp_{Z,t} - a_Z p_{Z,t+1})\left(a_z f_{Z,t}^B - f_{Z,t-1}^B\right)\chi_{t-1}^2$$
$$- (a_Z p_{Z,t+1} - rp_{Z,t})f_{Z,t}^B\sigma_t^2;$$
$$h_{Q_t,Q_t} = |\Omega_t|^{-1}\left[\left(a_z f_{Z,t}^B - f_{Z,t-1}^B\right)^2\chi_{t-1}^2 + \left(f_{Z,t}^B\right)^2\sigma_t^2\right];$$
$$h_{Q_t,Y_t} = |\Omega_t|^{-1}[p_{Z,t}f_{Z,t}^B\sigma_t^2$$
$$- (Rp_{Z,t-1} - a_Z p_{Z,t})\left(a_z f_{Z,t}^B - f_{Z,t-1}^B\right)\chi_{t-1}^2];$$
$$\mathbf{h}_t \equiv \left(\begin{array}{cc}h_{Q_t,Q_t} & h_{Q_t,Y_t} \\ h_{Y_t,Q_t} & h_{Y_t,Y_t}\end{array}\right) = [\text{VC}(Q_t,Y_t)]^{-1}$$
$$= \left(\begin{array}{cc}\kappa_{Q_t,Q_t} & \kappa_{Q_t,Y_t} \\ \kappa_{Y_t,Q_t} & \kappa_{Y_t,Y_t}\end{array}\right)^{-1};$$
$$|\Omega_t| = \det(\mathbf{h}_t);$$

with VC denoting the variance-covariance matrix. Since the signs of κ_{Q_{t+1},Q_t}, κ_{Q_{t+1},Y_t} and h_{Q_t,Y_t} depend on the signs of

$Rp_{Z,t-1} - a_Z p_{Z,t}$, $Rp_{Z,t} - a_Z p_{Z,t+1}$, $a_Z p_{Z,t+1} - r p_{Z,t}$, and $a_z f_{Z,t}^B - f_{Z,t-1}^B$, which are not unambiguous in the case of time-varying volatility, the sign of $\lambda_{3,t+1}$ is not unambiguous. In our numerical simulations, we could indeed observe both positive and negative values for $\lambda_{3,t+1}$. ■

Derivation of $E\left(\widetilde{Q}_{t+1} \mid \widetilde{Q}_t, V_t\right)$

We derive equation (3.20) in the following steps:

Step 1

Let x and y be two random variables with joint density function $f(x, y)$. Then

$$E\left(x \mid y = \widetilde{y}\right) = \int\limits_{-\infty}^{\infty} x f\left(x \mid y = \widetilde{y}\right) dx$$

where

$$f\left(x \mid \widetilde{y}\right) = \frac{f\left(x, \widetilde{y}\right)}{\int\limits_{-\infty}^{\infty} f\left(x, \widetilde{y}\right) dx}.$$

Step 2

Let x and y be two random variables with joint density function $f(x, y)$ and let $z = |y|$. The joint density of (x, z) is $g(x, z)$ where

$$
\begin{aligned}
g(x, z) &= 0 && \text{if } z < 0; \\
&= f(x, z) + f(x, -z) && \text{if } z \geq 0.
\end{aligned}
$$

Step 3

Let $\mathbf{y} = (y_1, y_2, y_3)'$ be normally distributed with $\mathbf{y} \sim N\left(\boldsymbol{\mu}, \boldsymbol{\Sigma}\right)$ where $\boldsymbol{\mu} = (\mu_1, \mu_2, \mu_3)'$. The density of $\mathbf{y}$ is

$$f\left(\mathbf{y}\right) = \frac{1}{\sqrt{2\pi \left|\boldsymbol{\Sigma}\right|}} \exp\left[-\frac{1}{2}\left(\mathbf{y} - \boldsymbol{\mu}\right)' \boldsymbol{\Sigma}^{-1}\left(\mathbf{y} - \boldsymbol{\mu}\right)\right].$$

Define $h\left(\mathbf{x}'; \boldsymbol{\Sigma}\right) = \exp\left(-\frac{1}{2}\mathbf{x}'\boldsymbol{\Sigma}^{-1}\mathbf{x}\right)$. Thus, we have

$$f\left(\mathbf{y}\right) = \frac{1}{\sqrt{2\pi \left|\boldsymbol{\Sigma}\right|}} h\left(y_1 - \mu_1, y_2 - \mu_2, y_3 - \mu_3; \boldsymbol{\Sigma}\right).$$

Step 4

Now we combine step 1 and step 3: Define the vector $\mathbf{z} = (z_1, z_2, z_3) = (y_1, y_2, |y_3|)$ with $\mathbf{y} = (y_1, y_2, y_3)'$ as in step 3. Let $g(\mathbf{z})$ be the density function of $\mathbf{z}$. From 2. step and 3. step we must have

$$
\begin{aligned}
g(\mathbf{z}) \;&=\; 0 \qquad\qquad\qquad\qquad\qquad\qquad\qquad\text{if } z_3 < 0; \\[2mm]
&=\; \frac{1}{\sqrt{2\pi\,|\mathbf{\Sigma}|}}[h(z_1 - \mu_1, z_2 - \mu_2, z_3 - \mu_3; \mathbf{\Sigma}) \\
&\quad + h(z_1 - \mu_1, z_2 - \mu_2, -z_3 - \mu_3; \mathbf{\Sigma}) \qquad\text{if } z_3 \geq 0.
\end{aligned}
$$

Step 5

Now we combine step 1 and step 4. The conditional density of y_1 give $y_2 = l_2$ and $|y_3| = l_3$ with $\mathbf{y} = (y_1, y_2, y_3)'$ as in step 3 is

$$
\begin{aligned}
f(&y_1 \mid y_2 = l_2, |y_3| = l_3) \\[1mm]
=\;& 0 \qquad \text{if } l_3 < 0; \\[1mm]
=\;& \frac{h(y_1-\mu_1,l_2-\mu_2,l_3-\mu_3;\mathbf{\Sigma})+h(y_1-\mu_1,l_2-\mu_2,-l_3-\mu_3;\mathbf{\Sigma})}{\int\limits_{-\infty}^{\infty}[h(y_1-\mu_1,l_2-\mu_2,l_3-\mu_3;\mathbf{\Sigma})+h(y_1-\mu_1,l_2-\mu_2,-l_3-\mu_3;\mathbf{\Sigma})]dy_1} \\[1mm]
& \qquad \text{if } l_3 \geq 0;
\end{aligned}
$$

Therefore, we obtain

$$
E(y_1 \mid y_2 = l_2, |y_3| = l_3)
$$

$$
\frac{\int\limits_{-\infty}^{\infty} y_1 \times [h(y_1 - \mu_1, l_2 - \mu_2, l_3 - \mu_3; \mathbf{\Sigma}) + h(y_1 - \mu_1, l_2 - \mu_2, -l_3 - \mu_3; \mathbf{\Sigma})]\, dy_1}{\int\limits_{-\infty}^{\infty} [h(y_1 - \mu_1, l_2 - \mu_2, l_3 - \mu_3; \mathbf{\Sigma}) + h(y_1 - \mu_1, l_2 - \mu_2, -l_3 - \mu_3; \mathbf{\Sigma})]\, dy_1}.
$$

It remains to compute these integrals.

Step 6

Rewrite $\mathbf{y} = (y_1, y_2, y_3)'$ as $\mathbf{y} = (y_a, \mathbf{y}_b')'$ with $y_a = y_1$ and $\mathbf{y}_b' = (y_2, y_3)$. The variance-covariance matrix of $\mathbf{y}$ can be written as

$$\Sigma = \begin{pmatrix} \Sigma_{aa} & \Sigma_{ab}' \\ \Sigma_{ab} & \Sigma_{bb} \end{pmatrix}.$$

Its inverse is

$$\Sigma^{-1} = \begin{pmatrix} \Gamma_{aa} & \Gamma_{ab}' \\ \Gamma_{ab} & \Gamma_{bb} \end{pmatrix}$$

with

$$\begin{aligned}
\Gamma_{aa} &= \left(\Sigma_{aa} - \Sigma_{ab}' \Sigma_{bb}^{-1} \Sigma_{ab} \right)^{-1} \\
\Gamma_{ab} &= -\Sigma_{bb}^{-1} \Sigma_{ab} \left(\Gamma_{aa} - \Sigma_{ab}' \Sigma_{bb}^{-1} \Sigma_{ab} \right)^{-1} \\
\Gamma_{bb} &= \Sigma_{bb}^{-1} + \Sigma_{bb}^{-1} \Sigma_{ab} \Sigma_{ab}' \Sigma_{bb}^{-1} \left(\Gamma_{aa} - \Sigma_{ab}' \Sigma_{bb}^{-1} \Sigma_{ab} \right)^{-1}.
\end{aligned}$$

It follows that

$$\int_{-\infty}^{\infty} h\left(y_1 - \mu_1, l_2 - \mu_2, l_3 - \mu_3; \Sigma \right) dy_1 = \left(\sqrt{2\pi \Sigma_{aa}^{-1}} \right) f \begin{pmatrix} l_2 - \mu_2 \\ l_3 - \mu_3 \end{pmatrix}$$

and

$$\int_{-\infty}^{\infty} y_1 h\left(y_1 - \mu_1, l_2 - \mu_2, l_3 - \mu_3; \Sigma \right) dy_1$$

$$= \sqrt{2\pi \Sigma_{aa}^{-1}} \left[\mu_1 + \Sigma_{ab}' \Sigma_{bb}^{-1} \begin{pmatrix} l_2 - \mu_2 \\ l_3 - \mu_3 \end{pmatrix} \right] f \begin{pmatrix} l_2 - \mu_2 \\ l_3 - \mu_3 \end{pmatrix}$$

with

$$f \begin{pmatrix} l_2 - \mu_2 \\ l_3 - \mu_3 \end{pmatrix} = \exp \left[-\frac{1}{2} \begin{pmatrix} l_2 - \mu_2 \\ l_3 - \mu_3 \end{pmatrix}' \Sigma_{bb}^{-1} \begin{pmatrix} l_2 - \mu_2 \\ l_3 - \mu_3 \end{pmatrix} \right].$$

Therefore,

$$E\left(y_1 \mid y_2 = l_2, |y_3| = l_3 \right)$$

$$= \frac{\left[\mu_1 + \Sigma_{ab}' \Sigma_{bb}^{-1} \begin{pmatrix} l_2 - \mu_2 \\ l_3 - \mu_3 \end{pmatrix} \right] f_1 + \left[\mu_1 + \Sigma_{ab}' \Sigma_{bb}^{-1} \begin{pmatrix} l_2 - \mu_2 \\ -l_3 - \mu_3 \end{pmatrix} \right] f_2}{f_1 + f_2}$$

$$= \mu_1 + \frac{\Sigma'_{ab}\Sigma^{-1}_{bb}\left[\left(\begin{array}{c} l_2 - \mu_2 \\ l_3 - \mu_3 \end{array}\right) f_1 + \left(\begin{array}{c} l_2 - \mu_2 \\ -l_3 - \mu_3 \end{array}\right) f_2\right]}{f_1 + f_2}$$

with

$$f_1 = f\left(\begin{array}{c} l_2 - \mu_2 \\ l_3 - \mu_3 \end{array}\right);$$

$$f_2 = f\left(\begin{array}{c} l_2 - \mu_2 \\ -l_3 - \mu_3 \end{array}\right).$$

Step 7

In our case, $y_a = \tilde{Q}_{t+1}$ and $\mathbf{y}'_b = \left(\tilde{Q}_t, V_t\right)$. Thus, $\mu_1 = E\left(\tilde{Q}_{t+1}\right) = 0$, $\mu_2 = E\left(\tilde{Q}_t\right) = 0$, and $\mu_3 = E\left(V_t\right) = \mu_t$. Denote the covariance matrix of $\mathbf{y}$ as

$$\Sigma_t = \left(\begin{array}{cc} \Sigma_{aa,t} & \Sigma'_{ab,t} \\ \Sigma_{ab,t} & \Sigma_{bb,t} \end{array}\right).$$

Furthermore,

$$f_1 = f\left(\begin{array}{c} \tilde{Q}_t \\ V_t - \mu_t \end{array}\right) = \exp\left[-\frac{1}{2}\left(\begin{array}{c} \tilde{Q}_t \\ V_t - \mu_t \end{array}\right)'\Sigma^{-1}_{bb,t}\left(\begin{array}{c} \tilde{Q}_t \\ V_t - \mu_t \end{array}\right)\right];$$

$$f_2 = f\left(\begin{array}{c} \tilde{Q}_t \\ -V_t - \mu_t \end{array}\right) = \exp\left[-\frac{1}{2}\left(\begin{array}{c} \tilde{Q}_t \\ -V_t - \mu_t \end{array}\right)'\Sigma^{-1}_{bb,t}\left(\begin{array}{c} \tilde{Q}_t \\ -V_t - \mu_t \end{array}\right)\right].$$

It follows that

$$E\left(\tilde{Q}_{t+1} \mid \tilde{Q}_t, V_t\right)$$

$$= \Sigma'_{ab,t}\Sigma^{-1}_{bb,t}\frac{\left(\begin{array}{c} \tilde{Q}_t \\ V_t \end{array}\right) f_1 + \left(\begin{array}{c} \tilde{Q}_t \\ -V_t \end{array}\right) f_2 - \left(\begin{array}{c} 0 \\ \mu_t \end{array}\right)(f_1 + f_2)}{f_1 + f_2}$$

$$= \Sigma'_{ab,t}\Sigma^{-1}_{bb,t}\left\{\left[I_{11} + G\left(\tilde{Q}_t, V_t, \mu_t\right) I_{22}\right]\left(\begin{array}{c} \tilde{Q}_t \\ -V_t \end{array}\right) - \left(\begin{array}{c} 0 \\ \mu_t \end{array}\right)\right\}$$

$$= \Sigma'_{ab,t}\Sigma^{-1}_{bb,t}\left[\left(\begin{array}{c} \tilde{Q}_t \\ -\mu_t \end{array}\right) + \left(\begin{array}{c} 0 \\ V_t \end{array}\right) G\left(\tilde{Q}_t, V_t, \mu_t\right)\right]$$

with

$$I_{11} = \begin{pmatrix} 1 & 0 \\ 0 & 0 \end{pmatrix}$$

$$I_{22} = \begin{pmatrix} 0 & 0 \\ 0 & 1 \end{pmatrix}$$

and

$$G\left(\tilde{Q}_t, V_t, \mu_t\right) = \frac{f_1 - f_2}{f_1 + f_2}.$$

In our example,[1]

$$\Sigma_{bb,t} = \begin{pmatrix} \kappa_{Q_t,Q_t} & \kappa_{Q_t,Y_t} \\ \kappa_{Q_t,Y_t} & \kappa_{Y_t,Y_t} \end{pmatrix},$$

with

$$
\begin{aligned}
\kappa_{Q_t,Q_t} &= (1+a)^2 \delta^2 + (Rp_{z,t-1} - a_z p_{z,t})^2 \chi_{t-1}^2 + p_{z,t}^2 \sigma_t^2 \\
\kappa_{Q_t,Y_t} &= (Rp_{z,t-1} - a_z p_{z,t}) \left(a_z f_{Z,t}^B - f_{Z,t-1}^B\right) \chi_{t-1}^2 - p_{z,t} f_{Z,t}^B \sigma_t^2 \\
\kappa_{Y_t,Y_t} &= \left(a_z f_{Z,t}^B - f_{Z,t-1}^B\right) \chi_{t-1}^2 + \left(f_{Z,t}^B\right)^2 \sigma_t^2.
\end{aligned}
$$

Define

$$\mathbf{h}_t \equiv \begin{pmatrix} h_{Q_t,Q_t} & h_{Q_t,Y_t} \\ h_{Y_t,Q_t} & h_{Y_t,Y_t} \end{pmatrix} = \Sigma_{bb,t}^{-1}$$

with

$$
\begin{aligned}
h_{Q_t,Q_t} &= |\Omega_t|^{-1} \kappa_{Y_t,Y_t} \\
h_{Q_t,Y_t} &= -|\Omega_t|^{-1} \kappa_{Q_t,Y_t} \\
h_{Y_t,Y_t} &= |\Omega_t|^{-1} \kappa_{Q_t,Q_t} \\
|\Omega_t| &= \det\left(\mathbf{h}_t\right).
\end{aligned}
$$

Therefore,

$$\Sigma_{ab,t}' \Sigma_{bb,t}^{-1} = \begin{pmatrix} \kappa_{Q_{t+1},Q_t} h_{Q_t,Q_t} + \kappa_{Q_{t+1},Y_t} h_{Q_t,Y_t} \\ \kappa_{Q_{t+1},Q_t} h_{Q_t,Y_t} + \kappa_{Q_{t+1},Y_t} h_{Y_t,Y_t} \end{pmatrix}' \equiv \begin{pmatrix} a_{t+1} \\ b_{t+1} \end{pmatrix}'$$

---

[1] Y_t is defined as

$$Y_t \equiv f_{0,t}^B - f_{0,t-1}^B + f_{Z,t}^B Z_t - f_{Z,t-1}^B Z_{t-1},$$

see Appendix B.

with

$$\kappa_{Q_{t+1},Q_t} = a_Z \left(R p_{Z,t-1} - a_Z p_{Z,t} \right) \left(R p_{Z,t} - a_Z p_{Z,t+1} \right) \chi_{t-1}^2$$
$$+ p_{Z,t} \left(a_Z p_{Z,t+1} - r p_{Z,t} \right) \sigma_t^2$$
$$\kappa_{Q_{t+1},Y_t} = a_z \left(R p_{Z,t} - a_Z p_{Z,t+1} \right) \left(a_z f_{Z,t}^B - f_{Z,t-1}^B \right) \chi_{t-1}^2$$
$$- \left(a_Z p_{Z,t+1} - r p_{Z,t} \right) f_{Z,t}^B \sigma_t^2.$$

∎

References

[1] H. Akaike. Fitting autoregressive models for prediction. *Annals of the Institute of Statistical Mathematics*, 21:243–247, 1969.

[2] R. Antoniewicz. *An empirical analysis of stock return and volume.* PhD thesis, University of Wisconsin, Madison, Wisconsin, 1992.

[3] R. Aumann. Agreeing to disagree. *Annals of Statistics*, 4:1236–1239, 1976.

[4] R.T. Baillie and R.P. DeGennaro. Stock returns and volatility. *Journal of Financial and Quantitative Analysis*, 25:203–214, 1990.

[5] R.A. Bansal, A.R. Gallant, R. Hussey, and G. Tauchen. Nonparametric estimation of structural models for high-frequency market data. *Journal of Econometrics*, 66:251–278, 1995.

[6] L. D. Blume, D. Easley, and M. O'Hara. Market statistics and technical analysis: The role of volume. *Journal of Finance*, XLIX:153–181, 1994.

[7] T. Bollerslev, R.Y. Chow, and K.F. Kroner. ARCH modeling in finance. *Journal of Econometrics*, 52:5–59, 1992.

[8] W.A. Brock, W.D. Dechert, and J.A. Scheinkman. A test for independence based on the correlation dimension. Unpublished manuscript, University of Wisconsin, Madison, WI, 1987.

[9] W.A. Brock and B.D. LeBaron. A dynamic structural model for stock return volatility and trading volume. Working Paper 4988, NBER, 1995.

[10] J.Y. Campbell, S.J. Grossman, and J. Wang. Trading volume and serial correlation in stock returns. *The Quarterly Journal of Economics*, 108:905–940, 1993.

[11] J.Y. Campbell and A.S. Kyle. Smart money, noise trading, and stock price behavior. *Review of Economics & Statistics*, LX:1–34, 1993.

[12] J.Y. Campbell and R.J . Shiller. The dividend-price ratio and expectations of future dividends and discount factors. *Review of Financial Studies*, 1:195–228, 1988.

[13] J.Y. Campbell and R.J. Shiller. Cointegration and tests of present value models. *Journal of Political Economy*, 95:1062–1088, 1987.

[14] P.A. Clark. A subordinated stochastic process model with finite variance for speculative prices. *Econometrica*, 41, 1973.

[15] J.H. Cochrane. Explaining the variance of price-dividend ratios. *Review of Financial Studies*, 5, 1992.

[16] T. Doan, R. Litterman, and C. Sims. Forecasting and conditional projection using realistic prior distributions. *Econometric Reviews*, 3:1–100, 1984.

[17] S.N. Durlauf and E.R. Hall. Measuring noise in stock prices. Working paper, NBER Working Paper, 1989.

[18] R.F. Engle. Autoregressive conditional heteroskedasticity with estimates of the variance of United Kingdom inflation. *Econometrica*, 50:987–1008, 1982.

[19] R.F. Engle and G. Gonzales-Rivera. Semiparametric ARCH models. *Journal of Business & Economic Statistics*, 9, 1991.

[20] R.F. Engle and C.W.J. Granger. Co-integration and error correction: Representation, estimation, and testing. *Econometrica*, 55:251–276, 1987.

[21] E.F. Fama. The behavior of stock market prices. *Journal of Business*, 38:34–105, 1965.

[22] E.F. Fama. Efficient capital markets: A review of theory and empirical work. *Journal of Finance*, 25:383–417, 1970.

[23] E.F. Fama. *Foundations of Finance*. Basic Books, New York, 1976.

[24] E.F. Fama. Efficient capital markets: II. *Journal of Finance*, 46:1575–1617, 1991.

[25] E.F. Fama and K.R. French. Permanent and temporary components of stock prices. *Journal of Political Economy*, 96:246–273, 1988.

[26] L. Fisher. Some new stock-market indexes. *Journal of Business*, 39:191–225, 1966.

[27] K.R. French and R. Roll. Stock return variances: The arrival of information and the reaction of traders. *Journal of Financial Economics*, 17:5–26, 1986.

[28] K.R. French, G.W. Schwert, and R.F. Stambaugh. Expected stock returns and volatility. *Journal of Financial Economics*, 19:3–30, 1987.

[29] A.R. Gallant, D.A. Hsieh, and G. Tauchen. On fitting a recalcitrant series: The pound/dollar exchange rates, 1974-83. In W.A. Barnett, J. Powell, and G Tauchen, editors, *Nonparametric and Semiparametric Methods in Econometrics and Statistics, Proceedings of the Fifth International Symposium in Economic Theory and Econometrics*, pages 199–240. Cambridge University Press, 1991.

[30] A.R. Gallant, D.A. Hsieh, and G. Tauchen. Estimation of stochastic volatility models with suggestive diagnostics. Working paper, Duke University, 1994.

[31] A.R. Gallant and D.W. Nychka. Semi-nonparametric maximum likelihood estimation. *Econometrica*, 55:363–390, 1987.

[32] A.R. Gallant, P. E. Rossi, and G. Tauchen. Stock prices and volume. *Review of Financial Studies*, 5:199–242, 1992.

[33] A.R. Gallant, P.E. Rossi, and G. Tauchen. Nonlinear dynamic structures. *Econometrica*, 4:871–907, 1993.

[34] A.R. Gallant and G. Tauchen. Which moments to match? Working paper, Duke University, 1994.

[35] C.W.J. Granger and A.P. Andersen. *An Introduction to Bilinear Time Series Model*. Vandenhock und Ruprecht, Göttingen, 1978.

[36] S.J. Grossman. On the efficiency of competitive stock markets where traders have diverse information. *Journal of Finance*, 31:537–585, 1976.

[37] S.J. Grossman and J.E. Stiglitz. On the impossibility of informationally efficient markets. *The American Economic Review*, 70:393–408, 1981.

[38] E.J. Hannan. Rational transfer function approximation. *Statistical Science*, 2:1029–1054, 1987.

[39] L.P. Hansen. Large sample properties of generalized method of moments estimators. *Econometrica*, 50:1029–1054, 1982.

[40] D.A. Hsieh. Chaos and nonlinear dynamics: Application to financial markets. *Journal of Finance*, 46:1839–77, 1991.

[41] C.T. Hsu and G.O. Orosel. The informational role of volume: A comment. mimeo, Department of Economics, University of Vienna, 1995.

[42] J. Karpoff. The relation between price changes and trading volume: A survey. *Journal of Financial and Quantitative Analysis*, 22:109–126, 1987.

[43] M. Kim, C. Nelson, and R. Startz. Mean reversion in stock prices? a reappraisal of the empirical evidence. *Review of Economics & Statistics*, 58:515–528, 1991.

[44] A.W. Kleidon. Variance bounds tests and stock price valuation models. *Journal of Political Economy*, 94:953–1001, 1986.

[45] C.G. Lamoureux and W.D. Lastrapes. Heteroskedasticity in stock return data: Volume vs. GARCH effects. *Journal of Finance*, 45:487–498, 1990.

[46] B. LeBaron. Stock return nonlinearities: Comparing tests and finding structure. Working paper, University of Wisconsin, Madison, 1988.

[47] B. LeBaron. Persistence of the Dow Jones Index on rising volume. Working paper, University of Wisconsin, 1992.

[48] S.F. LeRoy and W.R. Parke. Stock price volatility: Tests based on the geometric random walk. *The American Economic Review*, 999:981–992, 1992.

[49] S.F. LeRoy and R.D. Porter. The present value relation: Test based on implied variance bounds. *Econometrica*, 49:555–574, 1981.

[50] A. Lo and C. Mackinlay. Stock market prices do not follow random walks: Evidence from a simple specification test. *Review of Financial Studies*, 1:41–66, 1988.

[51] D.J. Lucas. Asset pricing with undiversifiable income risk and short sales constraints: Deepening the equity premium. Working paper, Northwestern University, 1991.

[52] R.E. Jr. Lucas. Asset prices in an exchange economy. *Econometrica*, 46:1429–45, 1978.

[53] N.G. Mankiw, D. Romer, and M.D. Shapiro. Stock market forecastability and volatility: A statistical appraisal. *Review of Economics & Statistics*, 58:455–477, 1991.

[54] T. Marsh and R. Merton. Dividend variability and variance bounds tests for the rationality of stock market prices. *The American Economic Review*, 76:483–498, 1986.

[55] A.I. McLeod and W.K. Li. Diagnostic checking ARMA time series models using squared residual autocorrelations. *Journal of Time Series Analysis*, 4:169–176, 1983.

[56] P. Milgrom and N. Stokey. Information, trade and common knowledge. *Journal of Economic Theory*, 26:17–27, 1982.

[57] D. Morse. Asymmetrical information in securities markets and trading volume. *Journal of Financial and Quantitative Analysis*, 6:461–464, 1978.

[58] D.B. Nelson. A note on the normalized residuals from ARCH and stochastic volatility models. Working paper, Graduate School of Business, University of Chicago, 1990.

[59] D.B. Nelson. Conditional heteroskedasticity in asset returns: A new approach. *Econometrica*, 59:347–370, 1991.

[60] J. Porterba and L. Summers. Mean reversion in stock returns: Evidence and implications. *Journal of Financial Economics*, 22:27–60, 1988.

[61] M. Richardson. Temporary components of stock prices: A skeptical view. *Journal of Business & Economic Statistics*, 11:199–207, 1993.

[62] M. Richardson and J. Stock. Drawing inferences from statistics based on multi-year asset returns. *Journal of Financial Economics*, 25:323–348, 1989.

[63] H. Sakai and H. Tokumaru. Autocorrelations of a certain chaos. *in IEEE transactions on acoustic, speech and signal processing*, ASSP-28:588–590, 1980.

[64] P.A. Samuelson. Proof that properly anticipated prices fluctuate randomly. *Industrial Management Review*, 6:41–49, 1965.

[65] T.M. Sargent. *Dynamic Macroeconomic Theory*. Harvard University Press, Cambridge, Massachusetts, 1987.

[66] G. Schwarz. Estimating the dimension of a model. *The Annals of Statistics*, 6:461–464, 1978.

[67] G.W. Schwert. Why does stock volatility change over time? *Journal of Finance*, 544:1115–1154, 1989.

[68] R.J. Shiller. Do stock prices move too much to be justified by subsequent changes in dividends? *The American Economic Review*, 71:421–436, 1981.

[69] R.J. Shiller. Stock prices and social dynamics. *Brookings Papers on Economic Activity*, 2:457–510, 1984.

[70] C. Sims. Macroeconomics and reality. *Econometrica*, 48:1–48, 1980.

[71] L.H. Summers. Does the stock market rationally reflect fundamental values? *Journal of Finance*, 41:591–601, 1986.

[72] G. Tauchen. New minimum chi-square methods in empirical finance. Working paper, Duke University, 1995.

[73] G. Tauchen and G. Pitts. Variability-volume relationship on speculative markets. *Econometrica*, 51:485–505, 1983.

[74] G. Tauchen, H. Zhang, and M. Liu. Volume, volatility, and leverage: A dynamic analysis. *Journal of Econometrics*, 74, 1996.

[75] S.J. Taylor. Modeling stochastic volatility. *Mathematical Finance*, 1994.

[76] H. Varian. Differences of opinion in financial markets. In C.C. Stone, editor, *Financial Risk: Theory, Evidence and Implications*, pages 3–37. Boston:Kluwer, 1989.

[77] J. Wang. A model of competitive stock trading volume. *Journal of Political Economy*, 102:127–168, 1994.

[78] K.D. West. Bubbles, fads and stock price volatility tests: A partial evaluation. *Journal of Finance*, 3:639–659, 1988.

[79] K.D. West. Dividend innovations and stock price volatility. *Econometrica*, 56:37–61, 1988.

[80] H. White. A heteroskedasticity-consistent covariance matrix estimator and a direct test for heteroskedasticity. *Econometrica*, 48:817–838, 1980.

List of Figures

List of Tables

Druck: Strauss Offsetdruck, Mörlenbach
Verarbeitung: Schäffer, Grünstadt

Vol. 361: C. F. Daganzo, Logistics Systems Analysis. X, 321 pages. 1991.

Vol. 362: F. Gehrels, Essays In Macroeconomics of an Open Economy. VII, 183 pages. 1991.

Vol. 363: C. Puppe, Distorted Probabilities and Choice under Risk. VIII, 100 pages . 1991

Vol. 364: B. Horvath, Are Policy Variables Exogenous? XII, 162 pages. 1991.

Vol. 365: G. A. Heuer, U. Leopold-Wildburger. Balanced Silverman Games on General Discrete Sets. V, 140 pages. 1991.

Vol. 366: J. Gruber (Ed.), Econometric Decision Models. Proceedings, 1989. VIII, 636 pages. 1991.

Vol. 367: M. Grauer, D. B. Pressmar (Eds.), Parallel Computing and Mathematical Optimization. Proceedings. V, 208 pages. 1991.

Vol. 368: M. Fedrizzi, J. Kacprzyk, M. Roubens (Eds.), Interactive Fuzzy Optimization. VII, 216 pages. 1991.

Vol. 369: R. Koblo, The Visible Hand. VIII, 131 pages.1991.

Vol. 370: M. J. Beckmann, M. N. Gopalan, R. Subramanian (Eds.), Stochastic Processes and their Applications. Proceedings, 1990. XLI, 292 pages. 1991.

Vol. 371: A. Schmutzler, Flexibility and Adjustment to Information in Sequential Decision Problems. VIII, 198 pages. 1991.

Vol. 372: J. Esteban, The Social Viability of Money. X, 202 pages. 1991.

Vol. 373: A. Billot, Economic Theory of Fuzzy Equilibria. XIII, 164 pages. 1992.

Vol. 374: G. Pflug, U. Dieter (Eds.), Simulation and Optimization. Proceedings, 1990. X, 162 pages. 1992.

Vol. 375: S.-J. Chen, Ch.-L. Hwang, Fuzzy Multiple Attribute Decision Making. XII, 536 pages. 1992.

Vol. 376: K.-H. Jöckel, G. Rothe, W. Sendler (Eds.), Bootstrapping and Related Techniques. Proceedings, 1990. VIII, 247 pages. 1992.

Vol. 377: A. Villar, Operator Theorems with Applications to Distributive Problems and Equilibrium Models. XVI, 160 pages. 1992.

Vol. 378: W. Krabs, J. Zowe (Eds.), Modern Methods of Optimization. Proceedings, 1990. VIII, 348 pages. 1992.

Vol. 379: K. Marti (Ed.), Stochastic Optimization. Proceedings, 1990. VII, 182 pages. 1992.

Vol. 380: J. Odelstad, Invariance and Structural Dependence. XII, 245 pages. 1992.

Vol. 381: C. Giannini, Topics in Structural VAR Econometrics. XI, 131 pages. 1992.

Vol. 382: W. Oettli, D. Pallaschke (Eds.), Advances in Optimization. Proceedings, 1991. X, 527 pages. 1992.

Vol. 383: J. Vartiainen, Capital Accumulation in a Corporatist Economy. VII, 177 pages. 1992.

Vol. 384: A. Martina, Lectures on the Economic Theory of Taxation. XII, 313 pages. 1992.

Vol. 385: J. Gardeazabal, M. Regúlez, The Monetary Model of Exchange Rates and Cointegration. X, 194 pages. 1992.

Vol. 386: M. Desrochers, J.-M. Rousseau (Eds.), Computer-Aided Transit Scheduling. Proceedings, 1990. XIII, 432 pages. 1992.

Vol. 387: W. Gaertner, M. Klemisch-Ahlert, Social Choice and Bargaining Perspectives on Distributive Justice. VIII, 131 pages. 1992.

Vol. 388: D. Bartmann, M. J. Beckmann, Inventory Control. XV, 252 pages. 1992.

Vol. 389: B. Dutta, D. Mookherjee, T. Parthasarathy, T. Raghavan, D. Ray, S. Tijs (Eds.), Game Theory and Economic Applications. Proceedings, 1990. IX, 454 pages. 1992.

Vol. 390: G. Sorger, Minimum Impatience Theorem for Recursive Economic Models. X, 162 pages. 1992.

Vol. 391: C. Keser, Experimental Duopoly Markets with Demand Inertia. X, 150 pages. 1992.

Vol. 392: K. Frauendorfer, Stochastic Two-Stage Programming. VIII, 228 pages. 1992.

Vol. 393: B. Lucke, Price Stabilization on World Agricultural Markets. XI, 274 pages. 1992.

Vol. 394: Y.-J. Lai, C.-L. Hwang, Fuzzy Mathematical Programming. XIII, 301 pages. 1992.

Vol. 395: G. Haag, U. Mueller, K. G. Troitzsch (Eds.), Economic Evolution and Demographic Change. XVI, 409 pages. 1992.

Vol. 396: R. V. V. Vidal (Ed.), Applied Simulated Annealing. VIII, 358 pages. 1992.

Vol. 397: J. Wessels, A. P. Wierzbicki (Eds.), User-Oriented Methodology and Techniques of Decision Analysis and Support. Proceedings, 1991. XII, 295 pages. 1993.

Vol. 398: J.-P. Urbain, Exogeneity in Error Correction Models. XI, 189 pages. 1993.

Vol. 399: F. Gori, L. Geronazzo, M. Galeotti (Eds.), Nonlinear Dynamics in Economics and Social Sciences. Proceedings, 1991. VIII, 367 pages. 1993.

Vol. 400: H. Tanizaki, Nonlinear Filters. XII, 203 pages. 1993.

Vol. 401: K. Mosler, M. Scarsini, Stochastic Orders and Applications. V, 379 pages. 1993.

Vol. 402: A. van den Elzen, Adjustment Processes for Exchange Economies and Noncooperative Games. VII, 146 pages. 1993.

Vol. 403: G. Brennscheidt, Predictive Behavior. VI, 227 pages. 1993.

Vol. 404: Y.-J. Lai, Ch.-L. Hwang, Fuzzy Multiple Objective Decision Making. XIV, 475 pages. 1994.

Vol. 405: S. Komlósi, T. Rapcsák, S. Schaible (Eds.), Generalized Convexity. Proceedings, 1992. VIII, 404 pages. 1994.

Vol. 406: N. M. Hung, N. V. Quyen, Dynamic Timing Decisions Under Uncertainty. X, 194 pages. 1994.

Vol. 407: M. Ooms, Empirical Vector Autoregressive Modeling. XIII, 380 pages. 1994.

Vol. 408: K. Haase, Lotsizing and Scheduling for Production Planning. VIII, 118 pages. 1994.

Vol. 409: A. Sprecher, Resource-Constrained Project Scheduling. XII, 142 pages. 1994.